# stewart & sally walton's
# fabulous home makeovers

## 100 projects for a more beautiful home

**southwater**

This edition is published by Southwater

Distributed in the UK by
The Manning Partnership
251–253 London Road East
Batheaston, Bath BA1 7RL
tel. 01225 852 727
fax 01225 852 852

Published in the USA by
Anness Publishing Inc.
27 West 20th Street
Suite 504
New York NY 10011
fax 212 807 6813

Distributed in Canada by
General Publishing
895 Don Mills Road
400–402 Park Centre
Toronto, Ontario M3C 1W3
tel. 416 445 3333
fax 416 445 5991

Distributed in Australia by
Sandstone Publishing
Unit 1, 360 Norton Street
Leichhardt
New South Wales 2040
tel. 02 9560 7888
fax 02 9560 7488

Southwater is an imprint of Anness Publishing Limited
Hermes House, 88–89 Blackfriars Road, London SE1 8HA
tel. 020 7401 2077; fax 020 7633 9499

© Anness Publishing Limited 1997, 2002

Publisher: Joanna Lorenz
Senior editor: Clare Nicholson
Photographer: Graham Rae
Stylist: Catherine Tully
Designer: Caroline Reeves

Previously published as *The New Home Decorator*

1 3 5 7 9 10 8 6 4 2

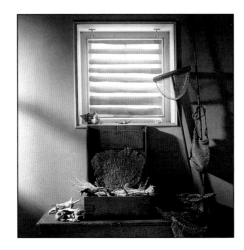

# CONTENTS

INTRODUCTION                                6

LIVING AND DINING ROOMS                     8

STUDIES AND HALLWAYS                        60

KITCHENS                                    92

BEDROOMS                                    134

NOVELTY ROOMS                               190

BATHROOMS                                   216

TEMPLATES                                   250

INDEX                                       254

# INTRODUCTION

DECORATION, COLOUR, AND DESIGN – never have they been more important than in the modern home as the twenty-first century approaches. Yet, while everyone wants a beautiful home, lives are busier and fewer and fewer people have the time or money to devote to intricate decorative schemes.

This book is an ideal starting point for anyone who is looking for ideas to brighten the home and add those individual touches that distinguish the exceptional from the ordinary. In it you will find decorative ideas for every room in the house, from living and dining rooms, through the kitchen – the most important room in the house – to studies, hallways and dens, so often neglected, and then on to children's rooms, bedrooms and bathrooms. Children's rooms, particularly, are very important and the right decorative detail can provide that missing amount of street cred for the lively teenager. As in so many things it is the willingness to devote time to the small touches that makes the difference and provides creative flair that will brighten your home.

*One of the easiest ways to change the look of a room is by making new lampshades. Interesting wall treatments are also a good idea, as they are often quick and economical.*

# LIVING AND DINING ROOMS

IMAGINE A ROOM FULL of light with cool, bleached tones and welcoming textures. Imagine it with bold strokes of colour, imaginative details and a hint of elegant understatement. Think beach-house, holidays, friends: relaxed, informal, calming. Now imagine this vision of cool as your own living or dining room.

An impossible, or impossibly expensive, dream? Not so. Transforming your living or dining room doesn't mean committing yourself to sweeping changes. Or paying a bevy of professionals to lay waste to everything from the light bulbs down. It doesn't mean discarding all your favourite things. It does mean using what you already have and concentrating on the details.

*A new-look laced chair provides a modern touch that will brighten any room in the house. Covers such as this can be changed to suit the room.*

Details are important, and in this chapter we look at ways in which an imaginative approach and quality execution can have an effect little short of miraculous. We have lots of ideas for both small and larger scale projects to point you in the right direction and loads of tips and shortcuts that can bring even the most professional-looking living/dining room decorating solutions well within anyone's reach.

Disguising a tired old lampbase or adding your own unique touches to unadorned cushions sound like minor changes, but when done imaginatively as part of a grand plan the effects can be stunning.

Equally, tackling bigger jobs is these days easier than ever. You can turn uninspiring or even scarred walls or floor surfaces into works of art. Wooden battens, painted and then fixed at regular intervals to a wall, add interest out of all proportion to the materials used and the skill needed.

Fledgling decorators can even make grand statements with upholstery and curtains — usually mentioned in the same breath as being both expensive and difficult — thanks to the staple gun and iron-on hem fix. These days you don't even have to sew.

That totally uplifting new living or dining room is just around the corner!

# SUPER SOFA

TRIM A PERFECTLY PLAIN sofa using only a strand of rope that curves gently down the edge of the arm and across the base. This type of decoration works extremely well in a white-on-white colour scheme because the eye is aware of the shape, but the embellishment doesn't jump out. Other types of trimming that could be used to add a stylish personal touch to your sofa are raffia edging, linen tassels and fringing.

## YOU WILL NEED

graph or plain paper

pencil

rope, the length of the area to be trimmed

clear sticky tape

scissors

dressmaker's pins

needle

strong sewing thread

**one** *Work out different designs for the rope on paper, to see what works the best; this style seemed sympathetic to the shape of the arm of the sofa and the lines of the seat.*

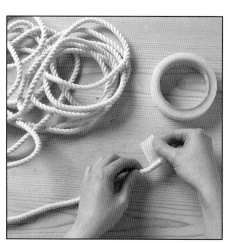

**two** *Bind clear sticky tape around the ends of the rope so that the ends do not fray once the rope is in position.*

**three** *Cut as close to the end of the tape as you can so that as little is left as possible, but it still holds the rope firmly. Pin the rope on to the sofa and hand-stitch in place.*

# CREAM TOPPING

MAKE A GRAND STATEMENT at the window by creating a pelmet with a curved edge trimmed with rope. The gentle wave of the pelmet gives a very gracious, elegant appearance to the treatment, which could, if you wish, be echoed in the edging of a loose cover on a chair or sofa. Another wonderful idea is to continue the pelmet right around the top of the room, so it acts as a wavy trim to the whole area. In this instance make sure the pelmet is the same colour as the ceiling so it doesn't interrupt the eye's progress. Pelmets can be any shape or size; experiment with pointed V's with bells on, castellations and the like. Cut the shape out of paper first, and pin it above the curtains to see what effect it will have upon the window and the room as a whole.

## YOU WILL NEED

tape measure
2 plates
paper, for template
pencil
pelmet fabric
dressmaker's scissors
interfacing
dressmaker's pins
needle and tacking thread
sewing machine
matching sewing thread
iron
rope
wooden batten
hammer and tacks or Velcro

**one** *Measure the window and decide on the dimensions of the pelmet. Allow an extra 5cm (2in) to fix to the batten. Use plates to make a template.*

**two** *Cut two pieces of fabric for the back and the front of the pelmet. Cut out interfacing to stiffen the pelmet, and pin the three layers together with right sides facing.*

**three** *Draw round the template on to the pelmet piece with a pencil. Pin the fabric just inside the outline.*

**four** *Cut out the scallops about 1cm (½in) from the outline. Tack along the edge, then machine-stitch.*

**five** *Trim the interfacing and clip the seam allowance so that the curves will lie flat when turned right-side out.*

**six** *Turn the pelmet right-side out and press the scalloped edge. Turn under the straight edge of the pelmet, then pin and machine-stitch.*

**seven** *Measure the scalloped edge, and cut a length of rope to fit. Experiment with design options for the rope; for example, you could use two different colours and weights of rope.*

**eight** *Pin the rope to the pelmet and hand-sew it in place. To attach the pelmet to the wall, use a slim batten of wood and nail the pelmet to it; alternatively, use Velcro to make the pelmet easy to remove.*

# STRING-BOUND LAMP BASE

STRING-BINDING IS A BRILLIANT way to disguise a tired old lamp base or to dress up a cheap chain-store buy. Look out for a lamp base with good proportions and a pleasing shape. There are many kinds of string to choose from, ranging from smooth, fine, waxy and white to fat, loose-weave brown twine, and all give different effects. You can paint the string afterwards if you want it to fit in with a room's colour scheme.

## YOU WILL NEED

glue gun with all-purpose glue sticks

china, glass or wooden lamp base

ball of string

scalpel or scissors

**one** *Heat the glue gun and apply a dot of hot glue below the flex on the bottom edge of the lamp base. Press the string in place. Apply a thin line of glue to the string and work it round the lamp base, keeping the string taut as you wind.*

**two** *Wind the string up around the base, dotting it with glue in key positions to hold the rows tightly together. When you reach the flex, cut the string. Apply a dot of glue on the other side of the hole and start the winding again with a new piece of string.*

**three** *Apply the glue at intervals as you wind and glue. Use plenty of glue when winding around concave shapes, as this is where the string may sag if it is not held firmly enough.*

**four** *At the top of the lamp base, apply an extra dot of glue and cut the string at an angle so that it lies flat.*

# MUTTON CLOTH SHADE

MUTTON CLOTH IS THE stretchy, tubular, knitted fabric that, although originally designed for wrapping meat, is generally used for cleaning. It can, however, be put to some more interesting uses. In this project, for example, it is used to cover an ordinary lampshade frame. The tube is opened out and pulled down over the bare lampshade frame. A second layer of fabric then covers the first and is fixed so that the edges roll over to create an interesting pattern. Finally a third layer of mutton cloth is pulled over to strengthen and protect the design.

### YOU WILL NEED
lampshade frame
tape measure
scissors
1.5m (1½yd) mutton cloth
dressmaker's pins
needle
matching cotton thread
embroidery needle
yellow embroidery thread

**one** *Cut a length of cloth three times the height of the frame. Pull the cloth down over the frame, so that you have just enough to roll under the bottom.*

**two** *Divide the remaining mutton cloth in two, then pull a second length down over the frame. Catch the middle of each side along the top and bottom of the frame and pin. The unpinned edges will roll up. Sew the first layer and the pinned section of the second layer securely to the frame.*

**three** *Pull the third length of cloth down over the frame and pin all around the top and bottom edges. Then stitch to secure the cloth in place.*

**four** *Cross-stitch around the top and bottom of the shade with a length of yellow embroidery thread to add a subtle finishing touch of colour to the shade.*

# CURVING ROPE DESIGN

A PATTERN IN ROPE makes a simple, textured wall finish, perfectly in keeping with today's trend for natural materials in interiors. Rope makes good curves, so the design can be as twisting as you like. For a small area or to make a focal point in a room, mark out squares and put a different, simple design in each square. You could also use the rope to create borders or frames within a room at dado-rail and picture-rail height for posters or paintings.

## YOU WILL NEED

scrap paper
pencil
spirit level
straight edge
rope
glue gun and glue sticks or strong adhesive
masking tape
craft knife
white emulsion paint
paintbrush

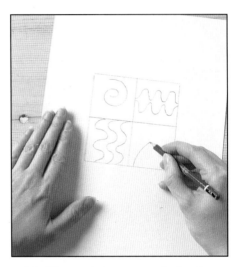

**one** *Plan and draw your design to scale on paper.*

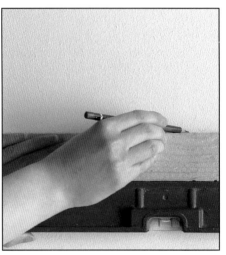

**two** *Transfer your design to the wall using a spirit level and a straight edge.*

**three** *Use a glue gun or other suitable adhesive to attach the rope to the wall. Use paint cans or other round objects to help you to make smoothe curves. It is easier if you wrap masking tape around it, and cut through the tape.*

**four** *Paint over the wall and rope with white emulsion paint; you may need a few coats to get an even finish.*

# LIFE'S LITTLE LUXURIES

CUSHIONS ARE THE PERFECT way to add a certain style, as well as an element of comfort, to your room. Here, the choice of natural tones and fabrics perfectly complements the simplicity of the sofa. Interest was added to the restrained look with decorative ties, looped buttons and a simple rope trim. If you want a change from the neutral colour scheme shown here, add splashes of vibrant colour with blues, reds, oranges and purples. Alternatively, blue and white always looks fresh and pretty.

**one** *For the rope-trimmed cushion cover, use a fine-gauge rope to experiment with different designs. When you are happy with the result, pin the rope on to the cover. Hand-stitch the cord to the cover, neatly finishing off the ends. Insert the cushion pad.*

**two** *For the cushion with ties, measure the cushion pad and cut one piece of cotton duck the depth of the cushion plus 1.5cm (⅝in) all round for seams, and a second piece twice the length plus 16.5cm (6½in) for turning. Pin, tack, press and sew the seams on the wrong side. Turn it right-side out.*

**three** *For the ties, cut six pieces of cotton duck 6 x 28cm (2¼ x 11 in). Fold each in half lengthways with wrong sides together and pin, tack, press and machine-stitch a 1cm (½in) seam round two sides. Clip the seams and corners. Turn the ties right-side out and slip-stitch the ends closed. Position the ties in pairs and topstitch securely.*

**four** *For the cushion with loops and buttons, measure the width and length of the cushion pad. Double the length and add 10cm (4in) for the flap opening, plus 3cm (1¼in) for seams all around. You will also need to cut a 7.5cm (3in) wide strip, the depth of the cushion plus seams. Cut the linen to this size and fold it in half.*

**five** *To make the piping for the button loops cut a length of linen about 2.5cm (1in) wide, on the cross. With wrong sides together, pin, tack and machine-stitch the fabric. Trim close to the stitching and, using a small safety pin, turn through to the right side. Press flat.*

**six** *Measure the buttons and cut the loops to the correct size. Turn over the seam allowance on the cover, then pin and tack the loops in position. Pin, tack and sew the interfacing strip for the back opening on the edge of the cover with the loops.*

**seven** *With the right sides together, sew a seam all around the cushion cover. Turn it right-side out and press. Mark the positions of the buttons with pins, and hand-sew them in place. Insert the cushion pad.*

# LIME-WASHED LAMP BASE

ONE OF THE MOST effective ways of updating a dull lamp is to give the base a fashionable paint finish and add a fresh new shade. Look out for a second-hand bargains in jumble sales or charity shops, then give them new life with a special paint treatment. This turned-wood lamp base has been given a limed look by applying and rubbing back two colours. The first, blue-grey coat of paint is rubbed off but remains in the grain and the grooves. The second coat of white paint is also rubbed back, leaving a transparent, lime-washed look.

### YOU WILL NEED

plain turned-wood lamp base

emulsion paint: blue-grey and white

paintbrushes

2 cloths

fine-grade sandpaper

**one** *Remove any surface finish on the base and sand it to a smooth finish. Then paint the bare wood with a coat of blue-grey paint.*

**two** *Before the paint has dried, rub it off with a cloth, leaving some colour in the grooves and grain. Allow to dry.*

**three** *Gently rub the decorative, raised parts of the lamp base with fine-grade sandpaper.*

**four** *Paint the whole lamp base with white emulsion. Rub off the paint before it has dried, using another cloth, and then allow to dry. Gently sand the decorative raised parts to create the lime-washed look.*

# COLOURED WOODEN BATTENS

SOMETIMES THE SIMPLEST IDEAS are the most effective. Strips of wood spaced on the wall at regular intervals can create an unusual and very dramatic look. Use them on a single wall or in smaller areas, such as the back of an alcove. The key is to keep the colours either toning or very contrasting and bold. If time permits, paint the top and bottom of the wood in slightly different shades of the same colour to add extra interest. The strips of wood used here are 5 x 2.5 cm (2 x 1in).

### YOU WILL NEED
tape measure

wood strips

pencil

saw

matt emulsion: blue and white

paintbrush

spirit level

drill, with masonry and wood bits

wall plugs

wood screws

ruler

**one** *Measure the height and width of the wall to make sure you will have equal spacing all the way up the wall. Cut the wood strips to the required length. Paint the wood strips; you could paint all three sides that will show in different colours, for a more interesting look, or in tones of the same shade, for subtlety.*

**two** *Use a spirit level to mark a guideline for the first strip, to make sure the wood is absolutely level.*

**three** *Drill holes in the wall and insert wall plugs. Drill holes in the wood and then screw the strip in place.. Mark out the position for the next wood strip; the space between strips must be absolutely even to create the right effect.*

# COLOUR-WASHED PARQUET

HERRINGBONE PATTERNS ON FLOORS give instant classical elegance, suggestive of the wonderful dark oak parquet floors found in large old houses. However, a fresher look is often wanted, yet with all the interest of the old floors; the introduction of a pale, soft colour lifts gloomy dark wood into the realms of light Atlantic beach houses or modern Swedish homes. To keep the interest of the grain of the wood running in different directions, paint each individual piece separately.

## YOU WILL NEED

marine-plywood, cut into manageable lengths

mitre saw

tape measure

sandpaper

matt emulsion paint: cream, blue and white

paintbrushes

matt water-based glaze

lint-free cloth

PVA floor adhesive

matt varnish

**one** *Make sure the floor is clean, dry and level. Mitre the edges of the marine-plywood strips, using a mitre saw. Remember that you must have left- and right-hand mitres in equal numbers. Measure your required length for the herringbone pattern and cut as many as you need for the floor.*

**two** *Smooth any rough edges with sandpaper. Undercoat all the boards with cream matt emulsion and allow them to dry completely.*

**three** *Mix up at least four variations of blue with a very slight tonal difference between them. Add a little matt water-based glaze to each, to delay the drying time. Thin one of the colours with water to make it even more translucent. Paint equal numbers of the boards in each colour.*

**four** *With the lint-free cloth, wipe off most of the paint randomly while it is still wet, so that the undercoat shows through. Wipe in the direction of the grain of the wood.*

**five** *For an even more weathered look, sand some areas of some boards when the paint is dry; this will give contrast when the floor is down. Lay the floor following the instructions for the Parquet project. Finally, ensure that the floor is dry and dust free, then seal the whole floor with at least two coats of matt varnish.*

# GEOMETRIC WALL-BOARD

YOU DO NOT NEED to be an artist to make a work of art for your wall and even make sure it's the right size and in complementary colours for the room! With a piece of MDF, a simple, repetitive design and a little time and patience, you can create a wall decoration at very little cost. A stencil is all that's needed and, if you stick to a design made of simple squares and circles, it is no problem to create your own stencil. Alternatively, it is worth looking at the commercial stencils available. There are so many designs to choose from, you are certain to find one you like.

## YOU WILL NEED

scrap paper

pencil

ruler

pair of compasses

MDF

tape measure

saw

emulsion paint: blue, yellow and red

paintbrushes

acetate sheet

craft knife

self-healing cutting mat

masking tape

stencil brush

small artist's brush

rubber

clear varnish

varnish brush

screw eyelets

picture-hanging wire

picture hook

hammer

drill, with masonry and wood bits (optional)

wall plugs (optional)

wood screws (optional)

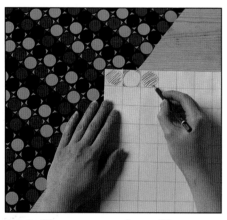

**one** *Choose your colours. You may consider complementing your existing furnishings. Plan out the whole design to scale on paper. Here, a wrapping paper design was used for inspiration.*

**two** *Cut the MDF to size, apply the blue base coat and allow to dry. Draw a grid of squares on the painted MDF. Use a ruler and compasses to draw the stencil on the sheet of acetate. Cut out the stencil carefully using the craft knife on a cutting mat.*

**three** *Tape the stencil over one of the squares on the grid. Stencil all the yellow circles and surrounds, then stencil the red circles and surrounds.*

**four** *Touch up any smudges with the artist's brush. When the paint is completely dry, rub out any visible pencil lines.*

**five** *Apply a coat of varnish. Attach the wall-board to the wall by inserting screw eyelets and stringing picture-hanging wire between them. Hammer in a strong picture hook and hang the board as you would a painting. Alternatively, drill holes in the wall and insert wall plugs, screw the board to the wall and fill and make good the screw holes.*

# DRAWING-ROOM SECRETS

JUST BECAUSE YOU INVEST heavily in some great curtain fabric, you should not feel committed to spending at least as much again on having it made up. This is a totally no-sew curtain and pelmet idea that could easily pass for the work of a professional! To work out how much material you need, just measure the drop and allow three times that length. The seams are all iron-on and the rest is done with a staple gun and string. It's hard to imagine that such an elegant draped pelmet could be put together without sewing a stitch. Follow the steps to discover the hidden secrets that lie behind this drawing-room window.

## YOU WILL NEED

striped fabric

scissors

iron-on hem fix (such as Wundaweb) or double-sided carpet tape (optional)

iron

2 wooden battens, window width, plus 30cm (12in) each side

spirit level

drill

wall plugs and screws

screwdriver

staple gun

string

**one** *Divide the fabric into three equal lengths, two for the curtains and one for the pelmet. Turn over the hems on both ends of the pelmet and one end of each of the curtains. Fix the hems with iron-on hem fix, or carpet tape if the fabric is very heavy. Fix the thin side of one of the battens to the wall so that the ends overlap the window equally – use a spirit level to check the position. Screw the other length of wood on to it at a right angle.* ➤

**two** *Starting at one end, staple the edge of one curtain to the front of the batten, inserting the staples vertically. Staple the other corner of the curtain to the middle of the batten. Most of the fabric will now hang loose in the middle.*

**three** *For the pleats, hold the curtain away from the window and find the middle. Staple this to the middle of the batten. Find the middle of the two loose sections. Staple them to the middle of the batten. Keep sub-dividing batten and fabric until you reach the pleat width you want. Repeat for the other curtain so that it matches.*

**four** *Fold the pelmet fabric in half lengthways and line up with the centre of the window. Starting at the centre, staple along one edge to the top of the batten, close to the wall. Lift the side drops and gather up the fabric at the corners. Put a row of staples under the gather so that the stripes line up with the curtain stripes below.*

**five** *Bunch up the fabric at each corner and tie it with string. Be aware of the way the fabric folds at this stage – you may need to practise folding and tying a few times until you achieve the desired effect. Staple the string to the batten. It won't show, so use as many staples as you like to make it secure.*

**six** *Tie another piece of string around the drop of the pelmet, about 30cm(12in) down. Tie it tightly, leaving enough string to allow you to tie another knot to raise this section to the top corner.*

**seven** *Pull the fabric up to the corner and tie the string ends around the first knot. Push the knots inside the remaining fabric to puff the front out. If necessary, add staples to hold this in place along the top of the batten. Finally, arrange the pleats and folds.*

# No-Frills Navy

BLOCK OUT THE LIGHT with these crisp, stylish navy blue curtains. Cotton duck is as heavy as denim, but to add firmness and thickness to the tops, you can use double-sided carpet tape to bond them together. This also means that you get a good fit with the large brass eyelets that are made for tent canvas and sails. You will need to buy fabric about one and a half times the width of your window plus an allowance of 5cm (2in) top and bottom to get perfect pleats. It is always a good idea to err on the generous side with curtains, so stretch the budget rather than the fabric on this project!

## YOU WILL NEED
double-sided carpet tape
craft knife
navy cotton duck
backing card
ruler
pencil
hole punch
hammer
brass eyelets
rigging wire, window width
2 wire rope grips
2 thimbles
pliers
drill
2 wall plugs and large hooks

**one** *Stick a length of double-sided carpet tape along the top of the fabric, just in from the edge. Peel off the top paper. Fold the top hem over the tape, smoothing as you go to ensure a crisp, wrinkle-free finish.*

**two** *Place the curtain on a sheet of backing card. Using a ruler and a pencil, mark the positions for the holes at 20cm (8in) intervals. Put the back part of the hole punch in position behind the fabric to make the first hole.*

**three** *Position the top part of the hole punch and bang it firmly with a hammer. Place the back part of the eyelet in the back part of the hole punch. Fit the middle of the eyelet through the punched hole.*

**four** *Place the top half of the eyelet on top of the bottom half. Position the tool provided with the eyelets and bang it firmly with a hammer. Continue positioning the eyelets at the marked intervals along the top of the curtains.*

**five** *Thread the rigging wire through the wire grip to form a loop. Place the thimble inside the loop and pull the wire taut. Using a hammer on a hard surface, bang the wire grip closed. You may also need to squeeze it with pliers.*

**six** *Drill holes and fix one of the hooks in the window recess. Loop the rigging wire over it. Thread the curtains on to the rigging wire through the eyelets.*

**seven** *Thread the other end through the wire grip as before, then attach to a hook. Screw the hook into a pre-drilled and plugged hole. This will ensure even pleats.*

# PRIMARY PLASTIC

THIN SHEETS OF OPAQUE, coloured plastic, which are available from art supply shops, make excellent lampshade materials. They are available in a range of colours, and the edges can be cut decoratively, with no need for seaming, and fastened in place with nuts and bolts. As plastic is a fairly rigid material, it does not require a supporting frame although you can use one for a template if you wish.

### YOU WILL NEED
brown paper
spray adhesive
sheet of red or yellow plastic
craft knife
cutting mat
pen
ruler
broad cloth tape
masking tape
scrap of wood
drill, with twist bit
nuts and bolts
shade carrier (optional)

*RED SHADE*

**one** *Enlarge the template and transfer it on to brown paper. Spray the back with adhesive and stick it on to a sheet of red plastic. Cut out the shade with a craft knife. Make a card template for the sawtooth pattern. Place it on the edge of the brown-paper pattern, on the plastic sheet, and draw round it to create a zigzag.*

**two** *Cut out the sawtooth border. Cut towards the outside edge every time. Remove the paper and fix the long edges of the shade together with cloth tape. Place a strip of masking tape along this seam. Place the wood block behind the seam, then drill three holes through the plastic. Remove the tape and screw in the nuts and bolts.*

*YELLOW SHADE*

**one** *Enlarge the template at the back of the book and transfer it to brown paper. Spray the back with adhesive and stick it on to a sheet of yellow plastic. Place on the cutting mat and cut out the shade using a craft knife.*

**two** *Overlap the two long edges of the shade and secure with a strip of cloth tape. Then place a strip of masking tape along this seam.*

**three** *Using a ruler, mark five equal divisions along the seam. Place a wooden block behind the seam and carefully drill a hole through the plastic at each mark. Start peeling off the tape at the top of the shade and screw in a nut and bolt each time a drilled hole is exposed.*

# $\mathcal{D}$RAPED DIRECTOR'S CHAIR

COMPLETELY DRAPED IN A slip cover, a folding director's chair loses its functional character and takes on the role of an armchair. Avoid complicated fitting by cutting a simple tabard-type slip cover, based on squares and rectangles that are just tied together. You can then put the cover straight on to the chair without ironing, since it can be removed and stored flat when the chair is folded away.

**one** *Measure: (a) from floor to top edge of back; (b) from top edge of back to back of seat; (c) length of seat; (d) width of seat; (e) from centre of wooden armrest to inside base of seat; (f) from centre of armrest to floor; (g) from front edge of seat to floor.*

**two** *Measure and draw the pattern pieces directly on to the fabric, with a seam allowance all round each piece. Cut out, then pin, tack and sew the pieces together following the diagram at the back of the book.*

**three** *Mark and cut strips of fabric to make ties of a finished size of about 2.5cm (1in) wide and 40cm (16in) long. Put right sides together and sew the long edges together. Then turn them out and slip stitch the ends.*

**four** *Assemble the tabard as a cross (see diagram). Slip the finished cover over the chair and knot the ties firmly.*

# *L*ACED DINING CHAIR

**TRANSFORM A DULL CHAIR** into a modern piece with added comfort and dramatic colour. These covers can be permanent or changed at whim. Any bright canvas fabric is suitable; economic cotton duck has been used here. The fabric must have a little body or you will need to add a backing fabric. Ticking, canvas, linen or duck are all suitable.

Self-cover buttons with cord loops or, for the more skilled, buttonholes are good alternatives to lacing eyelets. Loops and toggles or frogging give a military look, especially with a bright scarlet fabric.

## YOU WILL NEED

dining chair

measuring tape

foam or rubberized horse hair (to fit the back of the chair)

scissors

tape for ties

thin wadding (to fit the back of the chair)

upholstery tacks

felt-tipped pen

tissue or pattern-cutting paper

3m (3yd) of 130cm (50in) wide cotton duck

dressmaker's pins

sewing machine

matching thread

iron

safety pins

fabric marker

hole-punching tool

hammer

8 eyelets

eyelet pliers

3m (3yd) cotton tape

**one** *Measure the chair back for the size of the foam backing or rubberized horse hair. Cut the backing to size and attach it to the chair back with ties at the top and bottom.*

**two** *Cover the foam or horse hair loosely with thin wadding and secure the wadding with tacks.*

**three** *Lay the pattern-cutting paper on the seat and draw round it, adding a 4cm (1½in) seam allowance. Make a pattern for the front of the seat back.*

**four** *Decide how deep the skirt will be, then work out the dimensions for the back. The back panel incorporates a box pleat to allow easy removal (see diagram). Draw a pattern.*

**five** *For the skirt, measure the two sides and front of the seat, then add 30cm (12in) for each of the four box pleats. Add 4cm (1½in) to the depth as a seam allowance. Make a pattern.*

**six** *Lay the patterns on your material and cut out each piece. Take the back panel and pin, then stitch the central box pleat down to 4cm (1½in) from the top of the seat and press it.*

**seven** *Stitch the front panel to the top of the seat panel with the right sides together. Trim and press open all the seams as you go.*

**eight** *Stitch the front panel to the back at the top and sides. Hem the bottom edge of the skirt. Fold and pin the box pleats so they fall in the corners of the seat. Machine stitch the seat and skirt in place along the top edges.*

**nine** *Put the cover on the seat, close the back pleat with safety pins and mark where the eyelets are to be with a fabric marker.*

**ten** *Remove the cover. Using a hole-punching tool, make holes for the eyelets.*

**eleven** *Following the manufacturer's instructions, attach the eyelets.*

**twelve** *Put the cover on the chair and lace up the back with cotton tapes.*

CONTINUED OVER ➤

BACK

SEAT

EDGING

FRONT

# DINING CHAIR

THE EFFECT IS STYLISH and practical and yet needs no sewing skills. None of the usual difficulties caused by the need for washing of fitted covers apply, so you can capitalize on the sheer drama that is created by brilliant white. A generous quantity of fabric is the only essential; this project uses a king-size pure cotton sheet, which is ready hemmed, but you can use any wide, preferably washable, fabric that is soft enough to knot and tie.

## YOU WILL NEED
chair

fabric

sewing machine (optional)

**one** *You need at least twice, and preferably three times, as much fabric as the width of your chair. Hem the fabric, if necessary. Throw the fabric over the chair and centre it.*

**two** *Tuck the fabric down the back behind the seat of the chair. If the chair has arms, do this all round the seat, so that the cover doesn't pull when you sit on the chair.*

**three** *Sweep the fabric round to the back of the chair.*

**four** *Tie a knot, making sure that the fabric is an even length on both sides and that you have attractive folds and drapes at the sides. Try to tie the knot confidently in one go: otherwise the fabric can look tortured and may be crumpled. Remember that the fabric should cascade down from the knot.*

# PARQUET

GOOD PARQUET IS A very manageable kind of flooring. There are numerous patterns to be made from combining these wooden blocks. A good trick is to work out the pattern starting from the centre and make it as big a perfect square as you can; then lay a simple border to accommodate all the tricky outside edges. Parquet is often in oak but you could dye it with stain or varnish for a richer effect.

## YOU WILL NEED

pencil
string
ridged adhesive spreader
PVA floor adhesive
parquet blocks
timber length
matt varnish
paintbrush
fine-grade sandpaper

**one** *Make sure your floor surface is clean, dry and level. Find your starting point by stretching string from corner to corner as for tiles and draw guidelines on the floor. Using a ridged spreader, coat a small area of floor with adhesive.*

**two** *Apply parquet blocks to the adhesive. Use a length of timber laid across the blocks to check that they all lie flush. Repeat until the floor is covered. Seal the floor with two or three coats of varnish, sanding between coats.*

# GROOVY FLOOR

TONGUE-AND-GROOVE BOARDS look wonderful with a gleaming shine. Gloss paint or floor paint is durable and easily renewed if it's ever damaged. Use this floor in a room with a large window and enjoy the dramatic effect of the sun streaming across it. Gloss paint shows up detail, so it was a natural choice for these brand-new tongue-and-groove boards but, if you like the effect of the dramatic colour but have a an old, beaten-up floor, a matt finish would be more forgiving. To lay a new floor of this type, a perfectly smooth and level subfloor is vital.

## YOU WILL NEED
tongue-and-groove boards
hammer
drill, with pilot drill bit
flooring pins
pin hammer
nail punch
power sander and sandpaper
undercoat paint
paintbrushes
high-gloss floor paint

**one** *Slot the tongue-and-groove boards together and, using an offcut to protect the exposed tongue, tap the next board into place until it fits tightly. If the boards are warped, pin one end first and work along the board; in this way you will be able to straighten out the warp.*

**two** *To prevent the tongues from splitting, pre-drill pilot holes. Tap pins in gently, using a pin hammer, at a slight angle back towards the boards.*

**three** *Punch the pins in with a nail punch so the next board can butt up.*

**four** *When the floor is laid, and before finishing it, sand it, first with a coarse-grade sandpaper and then with medium-grade and finally with fine-grade. Always sand in line with the wood grain. With long, even strokes, in line with the boards, undercoat the floor. Leave to dry. Lightly sand again and paint with gloss paint.*

# JEWEL-BRIGHT ARMCHAIR

MANY ELEGANTLY SHAPED armchairs are disguised beneath several layers of ugly orange or dark brown varnish and dowdy upholstery fabrics. Once the covers have been removed and the old varnish has been sanded away, however, these chairs can be transformed instantly into desirable objects. Stretchy fabrics make it easier to achieve a neat, professional finish, but any upholstery fabric is suitable.

## YOU WILL NEED
armchair
medium-grade sandpaper
clear wax or silicone polish
rubber fabric
scissors
staple gun
rubber adhesive
paintbrush
hammer
upholstery tacks
thick artist's card

**one** *Remove all the old covers. Sand the varnish from the frame. Seal with clear wax or silicone polish. Using the existing cover pieces as patterns, cut the fabric to the size of the back rest, with a generous allowance to turn to the back surface. Stretch it over the back rest until it is hand-tight and staple it in place. Secure, in order, the top, bottom and sides, with one or two staples in the centre, before applying lines of staples to keep the fabric taut.*

**two** *Cut a piece of fabric to fit the back surface of the back rest and use rubber adhesive to stick the fabric to the chair so that it covers the staples and the turned-over edges of the first layer. Hammer a tack into each corner.*

**three** *For the cushion, trace its shape on to the card. Cut out and staple to the cushion. Wrap the fabric around the cushion, tucking in the corners neatly, and staple to the card. Attach a layer of fabric to the underside of the cushion (following step 2) and using rubber adhesive.*

# BOLD BLOCKS OF COLOUR

FOR THE BOLDEST LOOK of all, paint vibrant blocks of colour all over the walls to create an effect like a painting by the Dutch Cubist Piet Mondrian. Using a basic square grid, work across and up and down to create strong patterns and changes of colour. Although this example has been created in very brightly coloured paints, you could choose a more subdued or even subtle look, using complementary tones or much paler colours. Use this effect on all the walls in a room, if you're feeling brave, or confine it to one area, such as above a dado rail in a hall, for a less intense effect.

## YOU WILL NEED

spirit level

straight edge

pencil

scrap paper

emulsion paint in several colours

small and medium paintbrushes

masking tape

**one** *Draw a basic grid of squares directly on to the wall, using the spirit level, straight edge and pencil.*

**two** *Decide on your colours. Putting small samples together on a sheet of paper may help you to decide which ones work together best.*

**three** *Mask off the areas for the first colour. The blocks can be squares or oblongs, and they can turn corners. Use as many or as few squares of the grid as you like.*

**four** *Paint the blocks. Remove the tape immediately and leave to dry. Repeat the process for each of the subsequent colours in your scheme.*

# FLOATING FLOOR

WOOD-STRIP FLOORING IS a good way of creating instant elegance. It comes in a huge variety of finishes and lengths, so you can combine different woods without difficulty. Once you have mastered the principles of how to lay it, you can work out many different combinations and patterns. The main photograph shows walnut interspersed with wide, light-coloured maple boards. Alternatively, choose just one wood and lay it in different patterns. Laminated types of wood strip are generally pre-finished but others need to be sealed once they have been laid.

## YOU WILL NEED

cushioned underlay
(if necessary)

sticky tape

metal joint clips

hammer

wood-strip flooring

spacers

wood glue

saw

tacks and quadrant beading
(optional)

pencil

drill, with wood bit

**one** *If you are using underlay, unroll it and tape one end to keep it in place. Prepare all the boards of wood-strip by hammering the special metal joint clips into the groove on the underside of the board, along the tongued edge.*

**two** *Lay the first length, clips towards you, against the walls, using spacers. Glue the ends of butt-jointed lengths. Position the second row of boards, tapping them together with a hammer and an offcut, so that the clips engage in the groove of the second row.*

**three** *Cut the last board to width, allowing for spacers, and apply glue along its grooved edge. Insert packing against the wall before levering the strip into place. Tamp it down level with a hammer, using an offcut for protection.*

**four** *Replace the skirtings or tack lengths of quadrant beading to hide the expansion gap; make sure the skirting fits tightly against the floor.*

**five** *To fit a board around a pipe, mark its position and drill a suitably sized hole. Then cut out a tapered wedge, which can be glued back after fitting the board.*

# SPRIGGED CURTAINS

NATURAL CALICO HAS A lovely creamy colour, especially when the sun shines through it. However, it is usually used as a lining fabric, and this association can make it look unfinished. This stamped floral sprig lifts the humble calico into another dimension, giving it a sophisticated finish. Calico is prone to shrinkage, so wash the fabric before you stamp it and make up the curtains. The design for the calico stamp is in the template section at the back of the book.

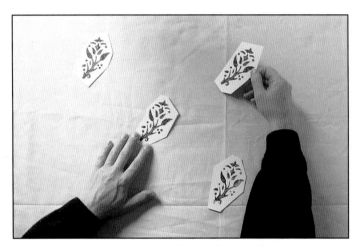

**one** *Lay the fabric out on a flat surface, such as a wallpaper-pasting table. Make several prints of the linocut stamp on scrap paper, cut these out with a scalpel and use them to plan the position of the motifs on the fabric.*

**two** *Decide on the distance between the sprigs and cut out a square of card with the same dimensions to act as a measuring guide. Use it diagonally, making a pencil mark at each corner over the surface of the fabric.*

**three** *Apply green ink directly to the edges of the linocut stamp. Fill in the middle of the stamp with dark blue ink. Make an initial print on a scrap of fabric to determine the density of the stamped image.*

**four** *Stamp the floral sprig on to the calico, using the pencil marks to position the base of the stamp. You need to apply gentle pressure to the back of the stamp and allow a couple of seconds for the ink to transfer. Don't rush; the result will be all the better for the extra time taken.*

# DISTRESSED FLOORBOARDS

OLD WOODEN FLOORS ARE often appealing because of their subtle variations of colour. Wood stains can help to imitate that look in only a few hours. The look of driftwood or weathered teak or other hardwood decking, like that of beach houses, is the aim. Achieve the outdoor look using three different wood dyes and a wash of white emulsion, diluted almost to water. This technique would give a bleached effect to any wood stain.

## YOU WILL NEED

nail punch

hammer

power sander and fine-grade sandpaper

wire brush

3 different wood stains of the same make

lint-free cloth or paintbrushes

rubber gloves

emulsion paint: white or cream

dry cloth

matt polyurethane floor varnish

**one** *It is important that floors have no sharp or protruding nails and so on, so knock in any you find with a nail punch before you begin. Remove old paint spills using a sander. Remember to change the sandpaper frequently, or you will damage the rubber seal of the sander.*

**two** *Brush the boards with a wire brush, along the direction of the grain, with the occasional cross stroke to give a distressed effect. Experiment with the stains, mixing colours together – a little should go a long way. Use scrap wood to test the effect before you commit yourself by staining the floor.*

**three** *With either a lint-free cloth or a paintbrush, apply the stain. This will stain anything porous, so wear rubber gloves and old clothes.*

**four** *Start by applying quite a generous quantity of stain, but rub most of the surplus off. Don't stop till you've finished the floor or there will be a definite line; keep the joins between areas random and avoid overlapping parallel bands of stain.*

**five** *It's better to do one thin coat all over and then go back to apply further coats. To give an uneven, weathered look you can work the stain into the knots or grooves with a brush.*

**six** *While the stain is still wet, brush on a wash of the diluted white or cream paint, about one part emulsion to four parts water.*

**seven** *Using a dry cloth, rub off surplus or apply more until you have the effect you want.*

**eight** *Apply at least two coats of clear varnish, sanding very lightly between coats.*

# CONTEMPORARY SHELF

ALTHOUGH NURSERY METHODS have been employed to decorate this shelf, the result is a decidedly sophisticated room feature. The shelf pattern has been cut into one half of a potato, with all the colours painted on at the same time, to allow one-step printing. A row of potato stamps like this has a three-dimensional quality, enhanced by the choice and positioning of the colours. This is an easy project to carry out, which has an effect far beyond its simple origins. Experiment with other colour schemes if you prefer, but test your pattern on a a scrap of paper first.

## YOU WILL NEED
ruler

potato

felt-tipped pen

scalpel

knife

gouache, poster or acrylic paint: red, light blue, dark blue, green and yellow

paintbrush

**one** *Measure the width of the shelf edge and cut the potato to fit. Draw the simple pattern shapes on to the potato. Cut down with a scalpel to outline the shape, then cut across with a knife to remove the background.*

**two** *Mix the paint, then apply each colour to a separate part of the design with a paintbrush.*

**three** *Begin printing the shelf edge, making the first print on the short side section that will be nearest the wall.*

**four** *Continue to apply the paint as before and stamp the pattern to cover all the shelf edges.*

# STUDIES AND HALLWAYS

STUDIES AND HALLWAYS ARE OFTEN the most neglected areas of the house, repositories for everything that cannot find a home elsewhere. No wonder that sometimes these spaces look a mess! They needn't — and you don't have to chuck everything out and start again. The clever way to transform these areas is to use what you already have.

The hall, in particular, is an important space. It provides that lasting first impression in any house and should give a hint of what lies beyond. There is little sense, after all, in having wonderfully light and bright rooms linked by a gloomy corridor crammed full of mismatched furniture and assorted fittings.

Studies and dens can be tricky to get right simply because they often need to double up as TV rooms, spare bedrooms, storerooms or playrooms. Decorated to reflect your personality, they can be enclaves for work and creative passions, while still retaining their multiple functions.

Mismatched though everything may be, you can still make everything look co-ordinated. Light fittings and lampshades, even the sun lounger that has seen better days, all can be given a fresh new look that makes them fit in perfectly.

*The style of lighting reflects the whole mood of the house. With a little imagination there are many designs that can be used for decorative lampshades at minimal cost.*

Imagine what you can put on the walls of these rooms! A big wall map given a coat of tinted varnish makes any study look like a million dollars. Wallpaper can be fun too, especially when you customize it your own way or even make your own. The Escher-inspired wall covering of grey and black geometric patterns looks sensational and is really very easy to do.

You can even press into service a photocopier, creating striking wall treatments at the push of a button. Take a favourite subject, make lots of photocopies, cut them out and glue them on to the wall. Can you imagine that anything so simple could look so good and achieve such successful decorative results?

# WILD WEST CHAIR

IF YOU HAVE AN old armchair of these robust proportions, it will lend itself to this fun treatment reminiscent of the pioneer days of the Old West. Make it over with animal-skin prints and leather fringing for a new and imaginative look, as well as a cosy and comfortable feel. You could also use leatherette for the cushion covers or blankets, which would still be in keeping with this chunky, masculine look.

## YOU WILL NEED
armchair
fun-fur or animal-skin fabric
upholstery needle
strong thread
tape measure
suede or leather
self-healing cutting mat
ruler
craft knife
PVA leather glue
double-sided tape
pencil
softwood block
studs
hammer
rubber or softwood scrap

**one** *Remove the seat cushions of the armchair and wrap in fun-fur or animal-skin fabric, leaving sufficient fabric to make a continuous flap the length of the cushion. Stitch securely. Decide on the length of fringing needed to decorate the inside and outside edges of the arms of the chair.*

**two** *Decide how deep you want the fringe on the leather or suede to be. Measure and cut the fringe with a craft knife on a cutting mat, leaving sufficient uncut material to make a hem. Apply PVA glue to the edge of the leather or suede and fold over the hem. Press it down firmly.*

**three** *Apply double-sided tape to the chair arms and stick on the fringing, matching it on both arms.*

**four** *Mark the positions of the studs with a pencil, using a block of wood to gauge the distance between each. Position the studs with your thumb, press gently and then tap with a hammer, protecting the stud with a scrap rubber or a piece of softwood.*

# SKEWBALD SHADE

A SKEWBALD PATTERN – brown patches on a white pony – is perhaps the boldest of animal-skin prints and always makes a strong style statement. It is very adaptable and can be used in a contemporary, minimalist room, a child's bedroom, a study, or to go back to its roots in a Tex-Mex decorating style. Brown parcel wrap is strong and makes satisfactory stencils; the shapes of the patches need to be irregular to imitate the unique character of a skewbald pattern.

## YOU WILL NEED

felt-tipped pen
brown parcel wrap
scalpel
cutting mat
spray adhesive
plain fabric lampshade
brown acrylic paint
paintbrush
glue gun with all-purpose
glue sticks
brown fringing

**one** *Draw irregular cloud-like shapes on brown parcel wrap. You need several small ones and a bigger one. Keep the shapes curved, with no sharp angles. Use a scalpel to cut out the stencils.*

**two** *Spray the backs of the stencils very lightly with adhesive and arrange them on the shade. Position the large shape to overlap the rim. Stencil the brown shapes on to the shade, working inwards from the edges and making sure the paint gets into the weave of the fabric.*

**three** *Stencil the larger shape right up against any edging strip, or over the rim of the shade. The pattern will appear more natural if you do it this way. Use the glue gun to stick the fringing around the bottom rim.*

# DUSTPAN TIDY

IF YOU HAVE TO excavate piles of paper, notebooks, lists and old letters every time you need a pen, then it is time to get the dustpans out! This project gives a new meaning to tidying up. Two metal dustpans can be spray-painted to match or in any colour combination and fixed together with bolts. Use the dustpans for stationery, a small in-and-out tray or, perhaps most suitably, for filing bills!

## YOU WILL NEED

2 metal dustpans

4 metal washers

enamel car spray paint: lime green and metallic blue

newspaper

G-clamp

2 pieces of corrugated card

pencil

drill, with metal bit

2 nuts and bolts

pliers

screwdriver

**one** *Spray one dustpan and two washers lime green and the others metallic blue. Protect your work surface with newspaper and build up the colour gradually with light puffs of paint. Leave to dry.*

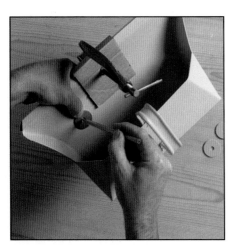

**two** *Clamp the dustpans together, protecting the paintwork with card. Hold the washers at the point where the dustpans meet and mark two equal positions with a pencil.*

**three** *Drill through the marks on both dustpans. Place a washer either side of a hole, hold the nut with pliers and tighten the bolt with a screwdriver. Repeat for the other hole.*

# EASTERN PROMISE

DIRECTOR'S CHAIRS ARE INEXPENSIVE, but because the back rest and the seat are made of cloth they are very comfortable. Plain canvas seats are the standard form, but by customizing you can create a fun and rather chic effect. Kelim fabric is very hard-wearing and has beautiful muted colours derived from traditional carpet designs, but any fabric that is strong and without too much 'give' can be used; tapestry, hessian, sacking or carpet are all suitable. For even more character, stain the frame of the chair to match the muted tones of the kelim.

## YOU WILL NEED

director's chair

wood stain and paintbrush (optional)

kelim carpet or fabric

dressmaker's pins

scissors

large darning or upholstery needle

strong darning wool

packet of chrome poppers (at least 6)

hammer

**one** *Remove the old seat and back of the chair. Stain the wood of the chair, if you wish. Choose the most decorative parts of the kelim carpet or fabric and pin the old fabric to it as a pattern. Carefully cut out new seat and back pieces.*

**two** *Thread the needle with the wool and neatly blanket stitch the edges to bind them.*

**three** *Fold over the edges of the back and fasten with chrome poppers, then slip over the uprights. Slot the seat back into position and secure firmly.*

# STANDARD PAINT CANS

NECESSITY REALLY IS THE mother of invention. This lamp was designed by a friend stuck in a remote village, who needed a good light to read by. The heavy lamp base is made from a large painted paint can filled with sand, while the shade is a smaller paint can drilled with a pattern of holes. The flex travels inside a curved copper plumbing pipe that is plunged into the sand. The graceful bend of the copper piping can be achieved only by using a special long spring used in the plumbing trade. If you know a friendly plumber, ask for help, otherwise a plumber's merchant should be able to bend the pipe for you. Ask an electrician to wire up the finished lamp for you.

### YOU WILL NEED

2.5 litre/½ gallon paint can
paint stripper (optional)
sandpaper
card
scissors
felt-tipped pen
drill, with size 6 twist metal bit
hammer and nail (optional)
metal file
pendant lamp fitting
matt-black emulsion paint
paintbrush
5 litre/1 gallon paint can
string
pipe-bending spring
3m (3yd) copper pipe
hack-saw
rubber grommet
silver sand to fill larger can

**one** *Strip off the paint or remove the label from the 2.5 litre (½ gallon) can, then rub down the surface with sandpaper. This will be the shade. Cut a strip of card the height of the can, then mark off three equal sections. Mark the other side in the same way but so that the marks fall halfway between the others. Use the strip to mark the drilling points around the can.*

**two** *Drill holes through all the marked points. Drilling through metal is not difficult, but if the drill bit slips, dent each mark slightly with a hammer and nail before drilling. Find the centre of the base of the can and drill four or five holes close together to make a larger hole. Use the end of a metal file to turn this into an even, circular hole that is the right size for a pendant lamp fitting.*

**three** *Roughen up the outside of the can with a file, smoothing the drilled-hole edges and scratching a texture into the surface. Paint the outside of the 5-litre (1-gallon) paint can matt-black. Paint the lid separately. Drill a hole for the flex near the base of the can. The pipe-bending spring will not be as long as the copper pipe, so attach a piece of string to one end of the spring. Mark the string at intervals so that you will be able to tell how far down the copper pipe the string is.*

**four** *Insert the spring into the pipe and start to shape the top third of the pipe into a semi-circle. You will not be able to bend the pipe in one go, so make small bends, bringing the spring back up the pipe as you work. Saw off the straight section at the end, so that the curve will go into the can. Then fix the rubber grommet to the end of the copper pipe.*

**five** *At this stage you need an electrician to thread the flex through the copper pipe and wire the fitting to it. The two halves of the fitting hold the shade between them. Drill a centrally positioned hole in the lid of the large can to take the copper pipe. Fit the lid over the base of the pipe and feed the flex out through the hole drilled near the base. Hold the lamp upright in the can and fill it with sand to ensure stability. Push the lid firmly on to the can.*

# Minimalist Chair

SLEEK BEECH AND CHROME chairs abound in interiors magazines – with price tags to match. This makes renovating old chairs a delightfully rewarding proposition. Most second-hand office-supply shops have a host of tatty typist's chairs, often with torn upholstery or in ghastly colours. Don't be drawn to a more modern chair that appears in a better state but has plastic-coated legs; metal legs look better when renovated.

## YOU WILL NEED
old typist's chair
scissors
screwdriver or bradawl
pliers
industrial rubber gloves
chemical paint stripper
2.5–5cm (1–2in) brush
wire wool
soap
medium-grade sandpaper
all-in-one stain and varnish
hammer
'domes of silence'
metal or chrome polish
soft, dry cloth

**one** *Start by cutting off excess fabric and foam. You need strong scissors with large plastic handles to avoid hurting your hands. Remove the fabric and upholstery staples from the back and underside of the chair. Use the screwdriver or bradawl for getting into tricky places and the pliers to pull out the old staples.*

**two** *Remove the castors and any other loose parts, to prevent them from being damaged by the paint stripper. Wearing the industrial rubber gloves, brush the paint stripper on to the metal chair frame. Leave for 5 minutes (or as long as the manufacturer recommends) and then wash off with wire wool and soapy water. Repeat until all the paint has been removed.*

**three** *Having removed the seat and back, make sure the surfaces are free of nails and staples. Sand the surfaces and edges of the seat and back until they are smooth and clean. Seal the wood with all-in-one stain and varnish, and leave to dry.*

**four** *Reattach the seat, back and castors. Use 'domes of silence' to cover any sharp bolts that might rip your clothes. Finally, polish the metal using a soft, dry cloth.*

# ANTIQUE MAP

MAPS ARE BOTH FASCINATING to study and extremely decorative, and this makes them wonderful for covering walls. Choose an up-to-date map for a child's room to maximize the learning possibilities. Elsewhere in the house, "antique" or old Ordnance Survey local area maps will look terrific and create an eye-catching focal point. You can easily distress a new map to give it an aged appearance. You could even paper a whole wall in maps – perhaps of geographically adjoining areas.

## YOU WILL NEED

tape measure
pencil
straight edge
spirit level or plumb line
map
wallpaper paste
pasting brush
fine-grade sandpaper
tinted varnish
paintbrush

**one** *Measure and mark guidelines for positioning the map on the wall, using a straight edge and a spirit level or plumb line. Paste the map to the wall as if it were wallpaper.*

**two** *Distress the map here and there by lightly rubbing it with sandpaper. Finish the ageing process by applying a coat of tinted varnish.*

# MATHS MONTAGE

THIS IS A FUN idea for adding interest to a plain wall. The numbers and mathematical symbols have been enlarged on a photocopier. It doesn't matter if the black becomes streaked with white as the number is enlarged: this enhances the hand-crafted look. It is most effective if you confine the montage to a fixed area, such as behind a desk, for maximum effect; just let the design fall away at the edges. You could also try musical notation behind a piano or shorthand characters in an office.

## YOU WILL NEED
craft knife
self-healing cutting mat
masking tape
wallpaper paste
pasting brush
artist's paintbrush
clear varnish
varnish brush

**one** *Photocopy the numbers and symbols from the templates at the back of the book and enlarge them to various sizes. Cut them out carefully with the craft knife on the cutting mat.*

**two** *Try out the design first by attaching the shapes to the wall using small pieces of masking tape; move them around until you are satisfied. Alternatively simply make a start and work out the design as you go. Paste the shapes on to the wall using wallpaper paste. Use the artist's brush to paste small and delicate shapes. Give the whole design a coat of varnish, to protect it.*

# ESCHER-STYLE WALL

INTRICATE 'THREE-DIMENSIONAL' designs, inspired by the *trompe-l'œil* drawings of the artist M.C. Escher, look stunning on a wall on which you want to make a real impact. The instructions for how to construct the design sound complicated but, in fact, once you have begun cutting out and assembling it, it soon becomes obvious how the shapes fit together. The beauty of Escher's designs is that all the components relate logically to one another in proportion and shape so that, once you have begun construction, the design practically assembles itself.

## YOU WILL NEED

scrap paper

pencil

metal ruler

paper: light grey, dark grey and black

craft knife

self-healing cutting mat

straight edge

spirit level or plumb line

wallpaper paste

pasting brush

clear varnish

varnish brush

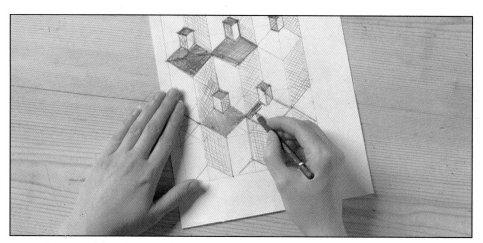

**one** *Plan and draw the whole pattern to scale on paper or refer to the diagram at the back of the book. Decide on the colours of paper you want to use; choose three tones of the same colour to achieve a three-dimensional effect. Measure the paper. Divide a sheet of the light grey paper into three.*

**two** *Measure in from the edge to the depth of the large grey triangle shapes that form the border and mark the points of the triangles.*

**three** *Draw the diagonals to make the triangle shapes. Cut out the large light and dark grey triangles and then the diamond shapes, using the craft knife on a cutting mat. You will find that, once you have cut one shape, you will be able to use it as a template for others, because of the way the shapes relate to one another.*

**four** *Draw the smaller light and dark grey diamonds that make two "sides" of the small "boxes". Cut out the smaller diamonds. Cut out the large and small black shapes.*

**five** *Using a spirit level or plumb line and straight edge, draw vertical lines on the wall the same width as the large grey shapes.*

**six** *Paste all the shapes into place using wallpaper paste and pasting brush. Smooth out any wrinkles with the palms of your hands. Give the design two coats of protective varnish.*

# ESCHER'S DECKCHAIR

DECKCHAIRS ARE CHEAP and widely available in several styles. The slings are usually canvas, available from high-street stores in a variety of brightly coloured plain and striped materials. Deckchair canvas comes in the correct width and with ready-sealed edges. To give an old deckchair a new lease of life use a pattern of stencils, or turn checks into a "three-dimensional" puzzle. This design is based on M.C. Escher's work and is made from a combination of positive and negative motifs.

## YOU WILL NEED
deckchair
deckchair canvas
scissors
spray adhesive
high-density foam
craft knife
self-healing cutting mat
ruler or set square
coloured tape
pencil
fabric paints: black and white
paintbrush
needle
matching thread

**one** *Remove the old sling, making a note of how it was fastened so that you can fasten it in the same way later. Using the old cover as a pattern, cut out the new fabric, allowing for hems along the top and bottom edges.*

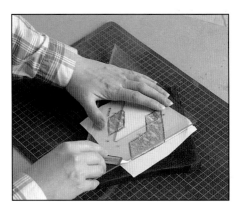

**two** *To make the two stamps for printing, photocopy the motifs from the back of the book to the desired size. Stick to the foam with spray adhesive. Cut round the design with the craft knife.*

**three** *Using the knife, chip away the zigzag shape between the dotted lines to leave two elements of the design standing proud. Remove all the foam that is not part of the "negative" design. It is helpful to mark the backs of the stamps with coloured tape to indicate which colour paint is used with which stamp. Repeat steps 3 and 4 to make the "positive" stamp.*

**four** *Using a ruler and pencil, draw parallel lines lengthways on the canvas, the distance between them equalling the full width of the design when the two stamps are put together (see step 7).*

**five** *Apply the black paint to the raised portion of one of the stamps.*

**six** *Applying light, even pressure, stamp the black design regularly within the grid lines.*

**seven** *Repeat with the white design. When dry, hem the top and bottom edges of the canvas, then fasten to the chair frame.*

# TRELLIS HANGING RACK

A GARDEN TRELLIS MAKES AN effective hanging rack. Extend the trellis to make regular diamond shapes and then frame it with wood to give a finished look. You could confine this idea to a small area or join a few pieces of trellis together to run the whole length of a wall. Put hooks on as many crossovers as you want, and collect decorative items, as well as the more mundane utilitarian objects, to make part of the display. Move things from time to time, so the display always offers something new to catch the eye.

## YOU WILL NEED

tape measure

pencil

length of garden trellis

hack-saw

2.5 x 2.5cm (1 x 1in) wood lengths

mitre block and saw or mitre saw

dowel length

wood screws

screwdriver

drill, with wood, metal and masonry bits

burnt-orange emulsion paint

paintbrush

wall plugs

wood filler

**one** *Measure the area you want to cover and mark out the area on the trellis. Cut the trellis to size with a hack-saw. Measure and cut the lengths of wood to make the frame. Mitre the corners using a mitre block or mitre saw. Screw the frame together.*

**two** *Mark the dowel into lengths and cut a notch in each length, for hanging hooks. Cut the dowel into lengths, using the mitre block or mitre saw.*

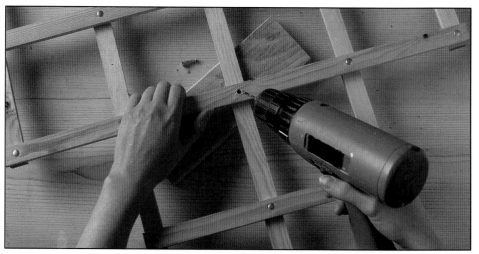

**three** *If the trellis is riveted at the crossovers, drill the rivets out. Position the dowel pegs on the trellis over the crossovers. Screw the pegs to the trellis. Paint the trellis and the frame with emulsion paint in your chosen colour. Burnt-orange has been used here.*

**four** *Drill holes in the wall with a masonry bit and insert wall plugs. Drill pilot holes in the trellis slightly smaller than the screws, to stop the wood from splitting, and then screw the trellis to the wall.*

**five** *Fix the frame around the trellis by screwing it on to the wall. Fill and paint over the tops of the screws and any gaps. When the trellis and frame are dry, give the whole hanging rack a second coat of paint.*

# Decorative Circles

**There is no reason** why the papers used for the walls and roofs of dolls' houses cannot be used on a full-sized wall. You could confine them to a limited area, such as below a dado rail or within panelling, or use them more extensively all over the wall. Here, the wall has been painted a complementary colour to the paper's and then circles have been cut out of the paper to reveal the colour behind.

## YOU WILL NEED

scrap paper

pencil

coloured pencil

doll's house paper

emulsion paint for the base colour

paint roller

paint-mixing tray

round template

craft knife

self-healing cutting mat

long metal ruler

wallpaper paste

pasting brush

paintbrushes

clear varnish

varnish brush

**one** *Plan and draw the whole design to scale on paper. Choose a paper with a small repeat pattern for the circles. Choose your base-paint colour to co-ordinate with the paper; it may help to paint swatches on scrap paper to see how well the colours work together.*

**two** *Paint the wall in the base colour. Decide on the size of the circles; you may have a plate, saucer or other round object of the right size, which you can use as a template. Decide on the spacing of the circles.*

**three** *Trim the paper, ready for pasting, using a craft knife on a cutting mat. Cut out the circles. Paste the paper to the wall as if it were wallpaper. Be especially careful of the edges where you have cut out circles, as these are delicate. If you prefer, draw guidelines for positioning the cut-out circles; otherwise, position them by eye. When the paste is completely dry, apply two coats of clear varnish, leaving to dry between coats.*

# *P*ULL-DOWN STOOL

**RESTRICTED SPACE IN FLATS** is common; you need to use every inch, and it is not easy to fit in extra seating, for example, by the telephone in the hall or other small area. Folding chairs are an obvious solution, but the problem of where to store them still arises. One answer is to adapt the clever folding brackets and hinges available from DIY stores, which are usually used for tables and shelves, to make a folding stool. Instead of a solid piece of MDF, you could could use dowel decking, such as that used in bathrooms. It is important that the stool is fitted to a masonry wall and not to a partition wall, which will not be able to take the weight, resulting in damage to the wall and person on the stool. Check the manufacturer's recommendations for fitting the right kind of screws and plugs.

## YOU WILL NEED

pair of folding brackets with screws

silver spray paint

medium-density fibreboard (MDF)

saw

pencil

ruler

pair of compasses or circular templates in three sizes

clamp

drill, with wood and masonry bits

jigsaw (optional)

medium-grade sandpaper

paintbrushes

yellow paint

clear varnish or lacquer

screwdriver

2 long screws and wall plugs

spirit level

**one** *Spray the brackets silver on a protected work surface.*

**two** *Cut the MDF to the right size for the seat: 30x45x20cm (12x18x8in) is normal. Draw a line down the centre of the seat.*

**three** *Place the brackets on the seat and mark their positions in pencil.*

**four** *With the compasses, draw three circles of increasing size. Alternatively, find three circular objects of suitable sizes to use as templates.*

**five** *Holding the seat firmly clamped to the work bench, drill a ring of holes just inside the pencil marks; this will allow you to cut out the circles with a jigsaw. If you are not confident with a jigsaw, take the seat to a hardware store or timber merchant who will cut the holes for you.*

**six** *Sand the holes to a smooth finish, both inside and on the top and bottom.*

**seven** *Sand off any pencil marks or fingerprints, to prepare the surfaces for painting.*

**eight** *Paint the inside of the holes yellow to highlight them.*

**nine** *Seal the seat with clear varnish or lacquer. A spray type is easy to use and will give a smooth finish.*

CONTINUED OVER ➤

**ten** *Screw the brackets to the seat. Hold the seat against the wall, which must be a masonry wall, and mark the position of the first hole with a pencil.*

**eleven** *Drill a hole using the masonry bit. Insert the wall plug and screw the seat loosely to the wall. Level the seat using a spirit level and mark the position for the second hole on the wall. Drill the hole, insert the wall plug and screw the other side of the seat to the wall.*

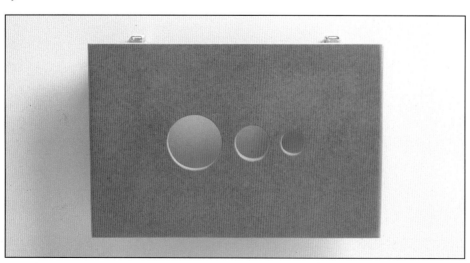

**twelve** *Check that the stool folds neatly against the wall.*

# SUN LOUNGER

SUN LOUNGERS COME IN various heights and with all kinds of additional features, but the fabrics, which are mostly garish prints and stripes, seem at odds with the smart tubular frames. Apart from the obvious solution of re-covering, using the existing fabric as a pattern, a smart alternative is to make a textural webbing cover. This fabric is hard-wearing and overcomes the problem of sagging. Re-covered in this way, the lounger offers both comfort and durability.

## YOU WILL NEED

sun lounger

chrome cleaner

soft cloth

tape measure

2 x 15m (16yd) upholstery webbing rolls

masking tape

pencil

scissors

6 packets of large eyelets

hammer

softwood block

needle

matching thread

6m (6½yd) cord or rope

**one** *Remove and discard the old cover. Thoroughly clean the metal frame with chrome cleaner and a soft cloth. Measure the width of the frame for the horizontal straps, and almost double this measurement so that the ends of the straps will very nearly meet in the middle.*

**two** *Position a couple of webbing strips with masking tape and work out how many strips you will need in each section of the frame. Cut the webbing to length and hem the ends.*

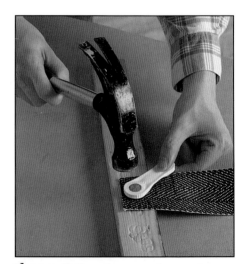

**three** *Follow the manufacturer's instructions for applying an eyelet to each end of the straps.*

**four** *Turn the lounger upside down, wrap the straps round the frame and fasten the ends together with cord or rope where they meet in the middle. Leave a gap wide enough for another strap near the hinges of the lounger.*

**five** *Starting at the foot, secure a vertical strap with an eyelet. Weave the strap under and over the double thickness of the horizontal straps until you reach the top. Secure the end with another eyelet.*

**six** *Near the hinges, thread another horizontal strap through the vertical ones, but wrap the ends round the two outermost verticals instead of round the frame.*

# Kitchens

KITCHENS ARE THE HEART of any home. So why not make yours look like it? You can, but remember — behind every outstanding kitchen is an outstanding decorator, for this is one room in the house where combining fun and function without breaking the bank requires ingenuity, and lots of it.

Look at what the kitchen has to be: work room; family room; storage room; dining room. Achieving all that in a functional, flexible, minimal-maintenance room AND making it a place where people feel good to be, depends on careful planning and lots of clever ideas.

The projects in this chapter present some of these ideas, many of which bring a new meaning to the word "recycling". The kitchen is where derelict and discarded objects come into their own — they not only look great but have a useful purpose as well!

The next time you visit the fruit shop collect some fruit boxes — with a lick of paint and a length of ribbon they make great stackable storage boxes. Transform a junk-shop-bargain window box into a striking and practical shelf for bottles, or suspend three metal garden sieves on lengths of chain to create a vegetable rack that's just brilliant.

*In any kitchen it is essential to be able to find the cutlery, and a decorative cutlery box in a striking modern design is a real asset.*

There's also a horticultural solution for the windows. To flood the kitchen with warm, glowing light, yet not with the stares of passers-by, try our wonderful blind made from a length of scrim edged with broads strips of hessian. With its cotton-reel pulleys it sounds a bit Heath Robinson-like, but that adds to the fun.

Once you've seen how much can be done with so little, your imagination will take over and no object, corner or surface will escape your attention. Your kitchen won't just be a better place to work, but an inviting room for family and friends, bright and cheerful enough to make your whole day!

# COUNTRY-STYLE SHELF

CONVEYING A UNIVERSAL MESSAGE the heart has been used in folklore art for centuries. Here a heart has been used to make a stamp that resembles a four-leafed clover. The smaller heart is a traditional solid shape that fits neatly along the edges of the shelf supports. The background colour was applied in three separate coats and rubbed back slightly between coats; a final lighter colour was applied over the top. When the shelf was dry, it was sanded with medium-grade sandpaper to reveal some of the grain and layers of colour.

### YOU WILL NEED
tracing paper

pencil

spray adhesive

high-density foam, such as uhholstery foam

scalpel

deep red emulsion paint

plate

paintbrush

**one** *Trace and transfer the pattern shapes from the template section. Lightly spray the shapes with adhesive and place them on the foam. Cut around the outline of the shapes with a scalpel. Cut out the single heart shape. First cut out the outline, then part the foam and cut all the way through.*

**two** *Use the stamp as a measuring guide to estimate the number of prints that will fit along the back of the shelf. Mark their position with a pencil. Spread an even coating of deep red paint on a plate.*

**three** *Make a test print of the clover-leaf stamp on a scrap of paper to ensure that the stamp is not overloaded with paint. Referring to the pencil guidelines, press the stamp into the paint and make the first print on the wood.*

**four** *Continue until you have completed all of the clover-leaf shapes. Try not to get the finish too even; this is a rustic piece of furniture. Finish off the shelf with a row of small hearts along the support edges, then add one between each large motif.*

# MEDITERRANEAN CRATES

WOODEN FRUIT AND VEGETABLE crates are much too good to be thrown away once their original contents have been used up, so rescue them from your local greengrocer and dress them up with colour and ribbon to make a great set of useful containers. The crates here work especially well, as they have a solid base that can be separated and used as a lid. These rustic Mediterranean crates look wonderful stacked with candles, tablecloths or other bright bits and pieces.

## YOU WILL NEED

3 wooden fruit or vegetable crates

sandpaper

pliers

wire cutters

staple gun (optional)

powder paint: red, blue and green

paintbrushes

100cm (40in) checked ribbon

scissors

**one** *Rub off any rough edges on the crates with sandpaper. Detach the base from one of them to be the "lid". Remove and replace any protruding staples if necessary.*

**two** *Mix the powder paints according to the manufacturer's instructions. Paint one of the crates red on the inside, blue on the outside, and green along the top edges.*

**three** *Paint the other crate green on the inside, blue on the outside, and red along the top edges.*

**four** *Paint the lid blue. Bind the six centre joints with crosses of checked ribbon, tied securely at the back.*

# WINDOW BOX SHELF

THIS ROUGH-HEWN RUSTIC box, stained dark brown, was found in a junk shop, and was probably in a garden shed thirty years ago. It is a good reminder not to write anything off until you have assessed its potential for here, painted and refurbished, it is both decorative and useful. Hang a window box on your kitchen wall to hold all the colourful bottles and jars that are usually hidden in a cupboard.

## YOU WILL NEED

wooden window box
sandpaper
emulsion paint: red, blue, green and white
paintbrushes
fine-grade wire wool
shellac button polish
drill, with wood bit
2 wall plugs and screws
screwdriver

**one** *Rub down the wooden surface of the window box with sandpaper. Paint it in bright colours, highlighting different parts in contrasting colours. Leave to dry.*

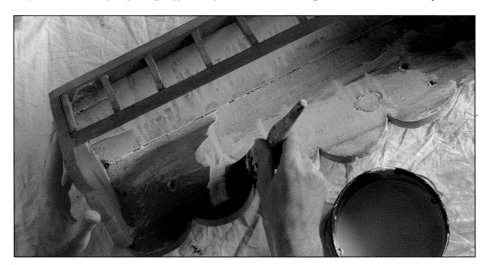

**two** *Mix white paint with water in equal parts and apply a coat of this all over the window box. Leave to dry. Rub back the white paint with fine-grade wire wool so that it just clings to the wood grain and imperfections.*

**three** *Apply a coat of button polish to protect the surface from stains and to improve the aged effect. Drill two holes in the back of the window box and fix it to the kitchen wall.*

# HANGING JAM JARS

THIS BRIGHT IDEA FOR getting double mileage out of kitchen shelves is borrowed from a tool shed. Woodworkers and gardeners line the undersides of their shelves with jam jar lids and then screw in jars filled with nuts, bolts, nails, screws and other useful things. Everything is kept tidy, on view and within easy reach. Fill your jars with biscuits, sweets, rice or different types of beans and lentils. You could even use smaller jars to create an unusual and inexpensive herb and spice rack.

## YOU WILL NEED

4 or more jam jars, with lids

kitchen shelf

pencil

bradawl

screws (no longer than the shelf depth)

screwdriver

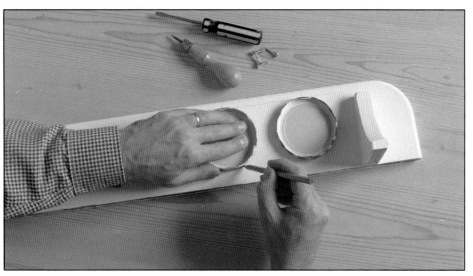

**one** *Arrange the jam jar lids along the underside of the shelf. There should be sufficient room between them for a hand to fit and sufficient depth for the jars to fit. Lightly mark the positions with a pencil.*

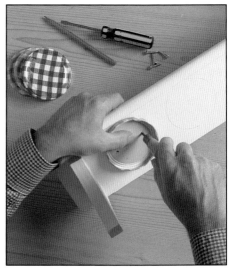

**two** *Use a bradawl to make two holes through each lid into the shelf.*

**three** *Screw the lids securely in place.*

**four** *Screw on the jars. It is easier to do this with the shelf on a work surface than with the shelf already hanging on the wall. Hang up the shelf.*

# VEGETABLE RACK

MOST KITCHEN ACCESSORIES seem to be made from practical but unattractive plastic, or high-tech and expensive chrome or stainless steel. This smart black vegetable rack is not the product of a design team from Tokyo, Milan or Paris – although it looks as if it could be – but is, in fact, three garden sieves (made either from wood and wire or galvanized iron) and a length of gatepost chain! Vegetables look enticing on display in a shop so why not store them in a place where they can be seen and appreciated? Suspend this rack in a kitchen corner so you can reach the vegetables easily when you need them for cooking.

## YOU WILL NEED

3m (3yd) chain, plus length to hang the rack from the ceiling

hack-saw

pliers

string

3 metal garden sieves

felt-tipped marker pen

scissors

masking tape

kitchen cloth

centre punch

hammer

drill, with metal and wood bits

15 "S" hooks (optional)

combine hook

ceiling hook and fixings (or long wall bracket)

**one** *Saw the chain into nine sets of twelve links, only sawing through one half of each link. Prise the links apart with pliers to separate the nine sections.*

**two** *Wrap a piece of string around one of the sieves to measure the circumference. Mark the measurement on the string. Cut the string to length.*

**three** *Fold the string into three equal lengths, marking it with the felt-tipped pen as you do so.*

**four** *Place the marked string around one of the sieves and stick masking tape on each third around the edge. The other two sieves need six marks – three around the top edge and three around the base edge. It is important to do this accurately so that the rack hangs level.*

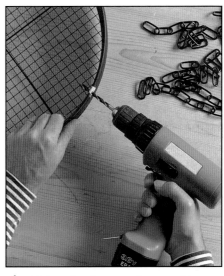

**five** *Place the sieves on a hard surface covered by a kitchen cloth. Use a centre punch with a hammer to dent the metal at each marked point.*

**six** *Using the dent marks as guides, drill holes on all three sieves. The dent mark should prevent the drill bit from slipping on the metal.*

**seven** *Insert "S" hooks into all the holes. Arrange the sieves in the order in which they will hang – the sieve with only three drilled holes goes on the bottom tier. Starting with the three-holed sieve, attach a length of chain to each "S" hook, adjusting the level to suit your needs by attaching the hooks at different links. To save expense, you could dispense with the "S" hooks and simply prise apart and then rejoin the chain links to attach the sieves directly.*

CONTINUED OVER ➤

**eight** *Clip the three top chain lengths together with a combine hook and add a further length of chain to suspend the rack from the ceiling. Find a beam for the ceiling hook as it needs to be strong to support the weight of vegetables.*

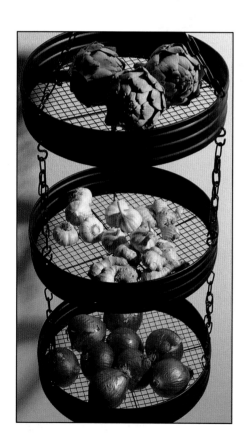

*The vegetable rack will look equally at home in a rustic interior or a stark, modern one.*

# Colourful Kitchen Chair

Introduce Provençal checks and stripes to the kitchen with soft furnishings; many kitchen chairs have detachable pads or padded seats, and the informality of the kitchen perfectly suits a jumble of frills, ties and prints. Consider the colours and patterns of your tablecloths and then, using bright colours, simple ginghams or stripes, mix and match. As an alternative, smart ticking stripes or pale pastels in sugar-almond colours would give this homely chair a sophisticated air.

## YOU WILL NEED

kitchen chair

tissue or pattern-cutting paper

pencil

thin foam

scissors

3m (3yd) of 137cm (54in) fabric

fabric marker

tape measure

ruler or set square

dressmaker's pins

sewing machine

matching thread

iron

ribbons or ties (optional)

**one** *Using the thin paper, draw the shape of the chair seat and cut this out of foam to form a cushion. On the wrong side of the fabric, draw the cushion shape again, adding a 2cm (¾in) seam allowance all round. Measure the depth and the circumference of the foam.*

**two** *Cut a bias strip of fabric to these measurements, with a 4cm (1½in) seam allowance all round. Attach the strip to the seat cover, by pinning and machine stitching the pieces together all around the edge, with right sides together.*

**three** *Decide how deep you want the skirt to be. The length is three times the circumference of the seat.*

**four** *From straight-grain fabric, cut one continuous panel or join two together. Hem the bottom edge and the two ends. Fold, pin and press the fabric into box pleats. When pleated, the skirt should be the same length as the sides and front of the cushion pad. Sew along the top edge, to secure the pleats. Attach the pleats to the bias-cut strip of the chair cover, with right sides together. Leave the back edge of the chair cover free of pleats, but turn up the hem allowance on the bias strip.*

**five** *Stitch ribbons or ties to the unfrilled edge and tie them around the back rest to hold the cover in place. Alternatively, cut ties from leftover fabric. Machine stitch them with right sides together, leaving a small gap. Trim the seam allowances and clip the corners. Turn the ties right-side out through the gap and slip-stitch the gap closed. Attach the self-ties in the same way as the ribbons.*

# CUT-ABOVE TILES

IF YOU'D LIKE TO RE-TILE your kitchen but are short of funds, this is the cheapest way of achieving the effect: simple photocopies cut into tile shapes, pasted to the wall and then varnished for protection. Find an appropriate motif that will fit neatly into a tile shape. Then you just need enough patience to cut out and paste the copies on to the wall. You could adapt the idea to other areas of the house: just change the motif to fit.

### YOU WILL NEED
cutlery motifs

pencil

metal ruler

craft knife

self-healing cutting mat

straight edge

spirit level

wallpaper paste

pasting brush

clear varnish

varnish brush

**one** *Photocopy the motif as many times as necessary. Draw a tile-shaped outline around the photocopies. Carefully cut the photocopies to the shape and size of a tile using the craft knife and cutting mat.*

**two** *Using a straight edge and spirit level, draw guidelines for positioning the tiles on the wall to make sure you put the photocopies on straight. Paste the photocopies on to the wall, making sure you cover all the guidelines. Allow to dry.*

**three** *Several coats of varnish will protect the wall and give a wipeable finish. Allow to dry between coats.*

# CUTLERY BOX

THIS PROJECT FUSES THE clarity of high-tech design with the starkness of surrealist sculpture – and it provides an ideal place to keep your cutlery at the same time! The stylish boxes look especially good in a modern kitchen, where chrome and stainless steel keep the lines crisp and the surfaces reflective. Make separate boxes for knives, forks and spoons and say goodbye to rummaging in the kitchen drawer.

### YOU WILL NEED

small silver-plated knife, fork and spoon, polished

3 metal boxes with lids

felt-tipped marker pen

coarse-grade sandpaper

metal file

metal-bonding compound (Chemical Metal)

craft knife

**one** *Bend the knife to a right angle halfway along the handle, over the edge of a table if necessary. Mark the position of the knife on the box. Roughen the parts of the knife and the box that will touch, with sandpaper and a file respectively.*

**two** *Mix the metal-bonding compound. Follow the manufacturer's instructions. Apply to the roughened area on the lid. The knife is fixed at this point, so the bond must be strong.*

**three** *Press the knife handle into position on the bonding. Use a fine instrument, such as a craft knife, to remove any excess bonding. Repeat these steps for the fork and spoon and their two metal boxes.*

# TROMPE L'OEIL LINOLEUM

LINOLEUM NOW COMES in many thicknesses, colours and patterns, and while it doesn't quite have the appeal of a beautiful classical floor, by cutting it into "three-dimensional" patterns and playing with slight colour variations you can create quite grand effects. Aside from the fact that lino is hard-wearing, water-resistant and probably one of the least expensive floor coverings, given this dramatic treatment, it can become the centrepiece of any kitchen. Rolls of lino and floor adhesive were used in this project, but you could also use self-glued tiles to make a floor reminiscent of a Venetian palazzo.

**YOU WILL NEED**

power sander, with fine-grade sandpaper

tape measure

pencil

paper

ruler

long metal ruler or straight edge

hardboard sheet

saw

linoleum rolls in different colours

craft knife

contact floor adhesive

**one** *You need a smooth, flat surface. If necessary, lay a marine-plywood or hardwood floor. Make sure that no nail heads are exposed, then lightly sand the floor.*

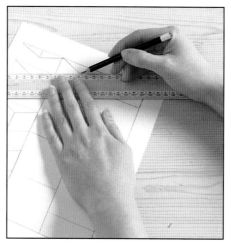

**two** *Measure the floor. To ensure a good fit, it's very important to work out the pattern on paper first, using the template.*

◄
**three** *Draw grid lines on the floor as a guide for laying the lino shapes. Draw each of the pattern shapes on a piece of hardboard and cut them out with a saw.*

**four** *Cut out the lino around the templates. Accuracy is important.*

**five** *Try out your pattern in pieces of lino and see if any need trimming. Number them on the back to fit them together more easily. Use contact adhesive to glue the tiles to the floor.*

# Vermeer-style Marble

You may be faced with a hardboard floor and long for the grandeur and impact of a marble one. Marbling is relatively easy to do. A wonderfully strong pattern is used here, taken from Vermeer's Old Master paintings. You may choose to do a simple chequerboard or even behave as if you had a huge slab of marble. Find a small piece of marble as reference (from the great variety of marbles to choose from) to create a realistic effect. This technique is not suitable for anywhere where there is a lot of moisture, but in the right place it can look amazing.

## YOU WILL NEED

tape measure

paper

pencil

ruler

black felt-tipped pen

white undercoat paint

paint roller

long straight edge, e.g. skirting length

artist's oil colours: black, light grey, dark grey, and silver

oil-based glaze

paintbrushes

lint-free cloth

bird's feather or quill

softening brush

dry cloth

fine artist's brush

black oil-based eggshell paint

white spirit

matt varnish

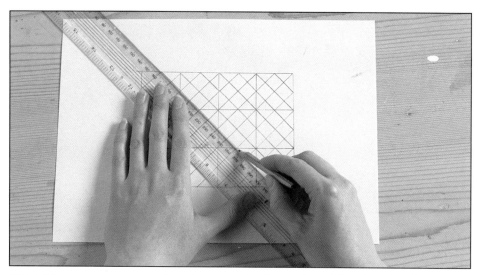

**one** *Measure your room, then draw a scale plan and a grid on it, using the template at the back of the book.*

**two** *Fill in your design, starting from the middle point of the floor plan and working out to the edges.*

**three** *You need a very flat surface, such as hardboard or marine-plywood. Undercoat the floor with a couple of coats of white paint.*

**four** *Draw the design on the floor in pencil. Put a small dab of black paint in each square that is going to be painted black.*

**five** *Add a little light grey oil paint to the oil-based glaze and apply it very thinly with a brush to all the squares that do not have black dots and will therefore be white "marble".*

**six** *With a lint-free cloth, soften the glaze while it is still wet to blend it and remove all traces of brush marks.*

**seven** *Dip a bird's feather or quill into a mixture of black paint thinned with a little oil-based glaze, and gently draw across the surface, to simulate the veins of the marble.*

**eight** *Use the softening brush to blur the outlines of the veining and blend them with the background. Wipe the brush regularly on a dry cloth to avoid smudges.*

**nine** *With a fine artist's brush, further soften the effect by adding white spirit, which will dissipate the lines. You can also add more colour of the same colour or a second colour, but remember to soften it again.*

CONTINUED OVER ➤

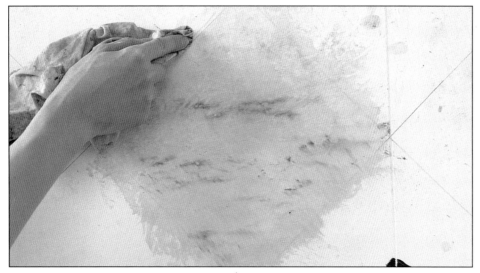

**ten** *Clean up the edges of the pencil squares with the corner of a dry cloth.*

**eleven** *Carefully fill in the black squares indicated by the black dots.*

**twelve** *Using a little dark grey or silver paint, applied directly on to a brush dampened with white spirit, soften the black in swirling motions so that it looks like slate. Finally, give the floor several coats of varnish.*

# WOODEN NOTICEBOARD

A NOTICEBOARD IS AN essential piece of equipment in a family kitchen and can also be an attractive display unit. This one makes a pleasant change from the utilitarian and rather dull cork type. Using a darker shade on the wooden strips and a lighter tone of the same colour on the wall produces a co-ordinated look. The slats used here are 2.5 x 2.5cm (1 x 1in), but you could use a different size if you wish.

## YOU WILL NEED

tape measure

wooden slats

pencil

saw

smoky-blue emulsion paint

paintbrush

spirit level

straight edge drill, with masonry and wood bits

wall plugs

wood screws

screwdriver

tacks

tack hammer

bulldog clips

**one** *Measure the wood to the correct length and cut as many pieces as you will need. Paint the wood in smoky-blue emulsion paint.*

**two** *Mark guidelines for attaching the slats using the spirit level and straight edge. Drill holes and insert wall plugs. Drill holes in the slats and screw them to the wall.*

**three** *Tap in tacks at intervals along the slats. Hang the clips from the tacks.*

# ON THE SHELF

EVERYONE HAS SHELVES somewhere in the home, but how many of us have thought of dressing them with different styles of edging? This project includes three different designs using natural materials that would be suitable for a kitchen. Experiment with anything and everything around the home, and you'll be surprised at just how innovative and exciting shelf edging can be. If you fix your trimmings with double-sided tape, they can be removed in an instant so, with very little effort, you can change the designs as often as you like.

## YOU WILL NEED
tape measure

string

scissors

sticky tape

red raffia

Chinese-language
newspaper

pencil

double-sided tape or
drawing pins

**one** *Measure the length of your shelf. Cut a piece of string about 5cm (2in) longer than the shelf, so it can turn around the corners. Cut more lengths of string, approximately 15–20cm (6–8in) long.*

**two** *Gather together bunches of about three lengths of string. Fold the bunches into loops and then pass the ends over the string and through the centre of the loop. Pull the loops taut to secure them. You can tape the string to the work surface if it makes it easier to work on it. Cut small pieces of red raffia and tie them into small knots between every two or three strands of looped string. Cut the raffia close to the knot.*

**three** *For the newspaper edging, measure the shelf. Cut strips the length of the shelf, and the depth you require. Fold each strip, concertina-fashion.*

**four** *Experiment by drawing different designs on to each folded strip. Cut out the edging shapes. Open them out and smooth them flat. Choose the shape that co-ordinates best with the style of decoration in the kitchen or reflects the shapes of the contents of the shelves.*

**five** *For the raffia edging, cut a piece of raffia the length of the shelf. Cut many short lengths of raffia.*

**six** *Loop them singly on to the main piece, as for the string edging. Tighten the loops and fill in any gaps. Trim the ends to one length to make an even fringe. Use double-sided tape or drawing pins to attach the trimmings to the edge of each shelf.*

# TUSCAN DOORWAY

WITH PATIENCE AND A little confidence, you can attempt a simple *trompe-l'oeil* wall decoration to create the atmosphere of a Tuscan country house in your own kitchen. The key to this rustic look is to layer the colours and then rub the layers back to reveal those underneath. The rest of the effect is created by masking off successive areas and finally adding simple, freehand "coach lines", so called because they are similar to the decorative lines on the liveries on horse-drawn coaches. It doesn't matter if your lines aren't perfect; it adds to the look. A final wash of watery ochre enhances the aged look.

### YOU WILL NEED

emulsion paint: cream, yellow, terracotta and green

paintbrushes in different sizes

paint roller

paint-mixing tray

pencil

scrap paper

set square or ruler

spirit level

straight edge

string

masking tape

hand-sander

brown pencil

**one** *Experiment with colours. You can pick quite strong shades as they will soften when they are sanded back. Apply the cream base coat.*

**two** *Wash over the base coat with a warm yellow paint.*

**three** *Draw your design to scale on paper using a set square or ruler.*

**four** *Measure and draw the straight lines on the wall, using the spirit level and straight edge.*

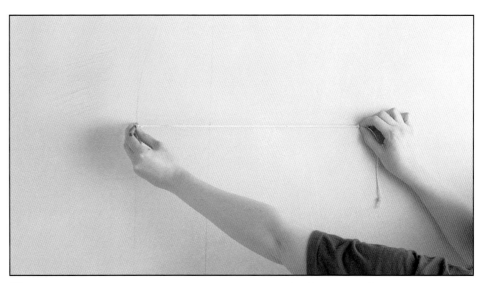

**five** *Draw the curve, using a pencil tied to a length of string in the same way as you would use a pair of compasses.*

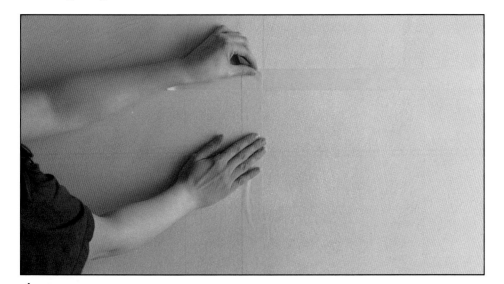

**six** *Mask off the areas to be painted in terracotta with tape.*

**seven** *Paint in the terracotta areas and immediately remove the tape.*

**eight** *Paint the other areas green, masking off if necessary.*

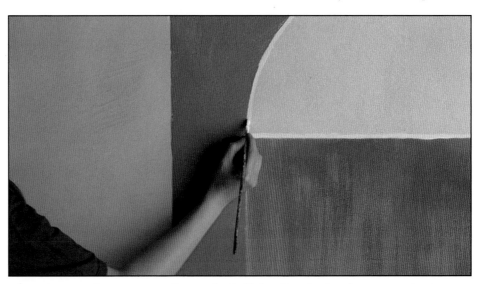

**nine** *Paint a thin cream outline around all the edges by hand.*

CONTINUED OVER ➤

**ten** *Lightly sand over the design, going back to the base coat in some areas and leaving others untouched.*

**eleven** *Wash over everything again with the warm yellow paint. Mask off the squares in the border. Paint the outlines and immediately remove the tape.*

**twelve** *Paint in all the outlines and immediately remove the tape.*

**thirteen** *Use the brown pencil to draw in extra-fine lines in the semi-circular "fan-light".*

# PAINTED BRICK "TILES"

THIN BRICK TILES ARE widely available and take on a new character when painted an interesting colour. You can arrange them in traditional brick-fashion or one above the other. Herringbone and basketweave patterns are also possible. As the right side is rough and the back is smooth, you can also have fun making patterns with the textures. Halved and quartered bricks make interesting borders and more complex variations on whole-brick designs. The colour you paint the bricks is all-important; the same design in white looks very different from ochre, for example.

## YOU WILL NEED

straight edge

spirit level

pencil

thin bricks

brick adhesive

hack-saw

pale yellow emulsion paint

paintbrush

grout (optional)

**one** *Use the straight edge and spirit level to draw guidelines for the positions of the bricks on the wall. Then, using adhesive and following the brick manufacturer's instructions, stick the bricks in place. Cut some bricks in half or in quarters with the hack-saw. Use the smaller pieces to make a border at dado-rail height.*

**two** *Give the bricks a first coat of emulsion paint.*

**three** *If you wish, grout the bricks and then paint over them and grout again. Otherwise, just give the bricks a second coat of paint.*

# HESSIAN & SCRIM BLINDS

THE NATURAL MATERIALS OF hessian and linen scrim are teamed up with bamboo canes to make this unusual Roman blind. The blind obscures the window effectively at night, and by day the sunlight streams through the scrim, making it appear almost transparent. The bamboo canes give the window a "potting shed" effect, and the ingenious pulley adds a Heath Robinson touch – not only does it look interesting, but it is also practical.

## YOU WILL NEED

hessian, to fit window
scissors
scrim, same size as hessian
stapler
6 bamboo canes
iron-on hem fix (optional)
iron
tape measure
saw
needle
matching sewing thread
12 x 1cm (¾in) brass rings
2 x 1cm (¾in) hinged rings
coat hangers
pliers
pencil
thin card
4 empty wooden cotton reels
4 screws
screwdriver
washers (optional)
string

**one** *Cut the hessian into four strips. Working on the sides first, fold a strip of hessian down the length of either side of the scrim to form a border, and staple the hessian and scrim together.*

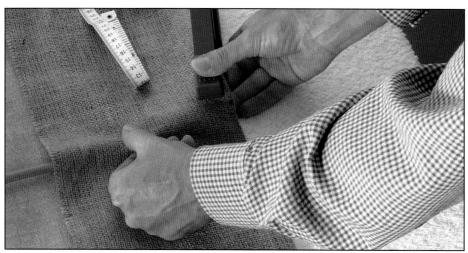

**two** *Divide the length of the drop by six to calculate the position of the bamboo canes. Saw the bamboo canes to fit the width of the window. Insert the first cane in position by holding it with the ends pushed up into the hessian border and stapling either side of it to make a channel. Repeat this process on the other side. Position the remaining canes in the same way, at equal intervals.*

KITCHENS 129

◄

**three** *Fold the hessian over the scrim at the bottom, as you did with the side, with a bamboo cane along its bottom fold. Staple this in place. Repeat this process with the top edge.*

**four** *If you are using iron-on hem fix, place it under the seam between the scrim and hessian and press it with a hot iron.* ➤

**five** *Stitch a brass ring to every point at which the hessian and scrim meet on a bamboo strut, including the bottom strut. Take the needle right through the fabric so that the thread goes around the bamboo each time for a strong fixing. Sew the two hinged rings, in line with the others, on either side of the blind top.*

**six** *Trim off overlapping hessian. If the fabric frays, insert some iron-on hem fix.*

**seven** *Cut five lengths of coat hanger wire from the longest part of the hanger – three lengths at 16cm (6¼in) and two lengths at 26cm (10in).*

**eight** *Using the photograph as a guide, draw the shape to hold the reels on to a piece of card. Then bend the shorter pieces of wire to that shape so that they will hold the reels.*

CONTINUED OVER ➤

**nine** *Bend the two longer lengths of wire into simple U-shapes to hold the blind, as shown.*

**ten** *Screw the first reel into the top right corner. Ensure that the screw heads are big enough, or add a washer to get a firm fixing. Align the loops of a pulley and a longer wire and fix both gadgets in place with the same screws. Screw the other reel and wire on the other side of the window, the same distance from the edge.*

**eleven** *Open out the hinged ring and use it to clip the blind up in position in the window.*

**twelve** *To thread the blind, start at the bottom and tie the string to the lowest ring. Thread up through the rings and over the pulleys. Do the same for both sets of rings.*

**thirteen** *Tie the two strings together about 15cm (6in) down from the corner pulley to prevent the blind from pulling up unevenly. Screw the last cotton reel into the wall for tying the string when you pull the blind.*

# BEDROOMS

IT DOESN'T MATTER WHETHER your fantasies run to the exotic, the minimal or the plain regal, the bedroom is one room in the house where you can indulge youself to your heart's content. After all it's your room so you can do what you like.

Whatever your tastes, our ideas rely more on imagination than money, more on practical inspirations than tool kit. And with our short cuts and great tips, decorating your bedroom won't put you to sleep. A good place to start is with the curtains. Tip number one: forget a curtain or fabric shop. Try instead a specialist sari shop. As soon as you enter you will be enveloped in colours you've only dreamt about. Imagine sunlight filtering through a window dressed with gossamer-light, deep-hued saris, the lightest breeze creating shivers of movement among the golden threads.

Or perhaps you fancy a bedroom of cool serenity and creative order. This calls for Japanese inspiration: simple, uncluttered lines, plain fabrics and pale colours. A garden trellis covered with heavy tracing paper becomes a translucent screen, providing privacy with the softest light — the perfect solution for windows that open on to a blank wall.

*A half-tester bed draped in cool white cotton adds romance and grandeur to any bedroom. It is simple and easy to create.*

Once again, side-step traditional shops and head straight to a painter's supplier — decorator's dustsheets are incredibly inexpensive and a perfect covering for a futon mattress. Making the base is easier than you think. To cast a subtle light on your Oriental dreams, make a bedside lamp from corrugated card and bamboo skewers.

Sleep like a king or queen under a faux-carved half-tester and canopy. Shop-bought decorative wooden and plaster mouldings provide the fanciful trimmings and the gilded finishing touches, and the effect of filigree wall panelling can be created by using nothing more than simple radiator cover panels.

# TRIPOD LIGHT

THIS CONTEMPORARY-LOOKING standard lamp appears quite delicate, but the tripod legs are very stable. The simple design makes it ideal for a Japanese-style room, particularly if a plain shade is fitted. The base consists of three pieces of wooden dowel fitted into angled holes drilled in a circle of wood. The frame of the shade is covered with butter muslin. The lamp is assembled by screwing a lamp fitting to the wooden disc, over a central hole through which the flex passes.

## YOU WILL NEED

dark oak wood stain

3 x 1m (1yd) lengths of wooden dowel

soft cloth

pencil

pair of compasses (optional)

square piece of wood

clamp

2 scraps of wood

coping saw

drill, with twist bit

craft knife or scalpel

wood glue

tape measure

large cylindrical shade frame

dressmaker's scissors

3m (3yd) unbleached butter muslin

dressmaker's pins

rust-coloured 4-ply wool

darning needle

shade carrier

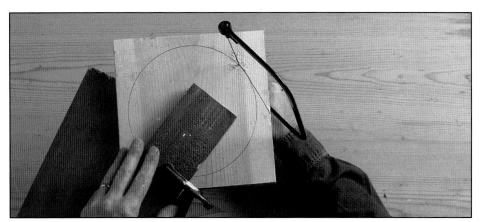

**one** *Rub the wood stain into the dowel with the cloth. Draw an 18cm (7in) diameter circle on the square of wood, then clamp it ready for sawing. Protecting it from the clamp with scraps of wood. Saw in from the edge at an angle and follow the curve with the blade. Move the wood around so that you can saw comfortably.*

**two** *Using a drill bit that is marginally narrower than the dowel, drill three angled holes through the wood circle. To do this, hold the drill directly above the centre, then tilt it slightly towards the edge, the angle will then be correct.*

**three** *Shave the ends of the lengths of dowel slightly with a craft knife or scalpel, apply wood glue and then push them into the drilled holes. Apply glue to the lengths of dowel where they intersect. Allow to dry. To cover the frame, measure around the circumference and height. Cut a double thickness of muslin 10cm (4in) wider than the height of the shade and long enough to fit around it, with an extra 4cm (1½in) as a seam allowance. Pin one end of the muslin along a strut, leaving 2cm (¾in) at each end for a seam, and gathering the fabric slightly as you go.*

**four** *Pin the muslin along the next strut and sew in place using blanket stitch. To sew blanket stitch, insert the needle behind the strut and pull it out in front. Do not pull the wool through. Take the needle through the loop of wool, then pull the wool tight. Continue stitching the muslin to each strut in the same way until you reach the first pinned seam. When you reach the final strut, join the two edges and stitch them together, still using blanket stitch.*

**five** *Finish off the top and bottom of the shade by rolling the edges around the wire frame, then pin and stitch them in place. Ask an electrician to attach the light fittings to the tripod, then place the shade on the carrier.*

# JAPANESE SCREEN

THIS SCREEN IS THE perfect treatment for a minimalist room scheme. It lets you hide from the outside world, yet you can still benefit from the light filtering through. The screen is made from a simple wooden garden trellis, painted matt black, with heavyweight tracing paper stapled behind it. You can cut the trellis to fit your window recess, but always do it to the nearest square so it looks balanced. The paper is stapled behind the struts.

## YOU WILL NEED

garden trellis
blackboard paint
paintbrush
heavyweight tracing paper
staple gun
craft knife
red emulsion paint
drill, with wood bit
2 eyelets
tape measure
wire coat hanger
wire cutters
pliers
2 picture hooks

**one** *Paint the trellis black and leave to dry. Blackboard paint creates a perfectly matt finish, but other matt or gloss paints can be used. Staple sheets of tracing paper on to the back of the trellis. If necessary, trim the tracing paper with a craft knife so that no overlaps or joins are visible from the front. It must look like a single sheet.*

**two** *For added interest, paint one square red and leave to dry. Drill a very fine hole in the top of the trellis, at the first strut in from each end.*

**three** *Screw an eyelet into each hole. Measure the length of the window to determine how long the hooks for hanging should be. The base of the screen should touch the window frame below. Cut two pieces of coat-hanger wire to the correct length for the hooks, then hang the screen on these from picture rail hooks.*

# JAPANESE FUTON

THIS STYLISH AND UNCLUTTERED bedroom exudes a typically Japanese sense of simplicity, order and tranquillity. Wooden pallets were used to make the bed base. These come in different sizes, but they can be sawn down and stacked to get the right size. The beautiful cream cotton bedcover is, unbelievably, a decorator's dustsheet, decorated with knotted cords. Dustsheets like this are incredibly cheap, so you can have the minimalist look for a minimal outlay. Just add a pillow and a cushion – and sleep well!

## YOU WILL NEED

wooden pallets
medium- and fine-grade sandpaper
light-coloured woodstain
paintbrush
2m (2yd) black cotton cord
scissors
needle
thread
decorator's dustsheet
2 black tassels
square cream-coloured cushion

**one** *Rub down the wooden pallets, using first medium-grade, then fine-grade sandpaper. Apply a coat of light-coloured woodstain to seal and colour the wood. Lay the pallets on the floor to make a bed base.*

**two** *Cut six 30cm (12in) lengths of black cotton cord. Make each length into a loop tied with a reef knot.*

**three** *Slip-stitch the knotted cords on to the dustsheet to make three rows of two cords down the centre of the bed. Spread the dustsheet on the bed and fold it neatly over the pillows. Sew two black tassels on to the cushion and place it on the pillows. Tuck the dustsheet under the mattress all the way around the bed.*

# STAMPS AND DRY BRUSH

SOMETIMES, WITH A ROOM that has unusual furnishings, it is worthwhile giving it a further distinctive style, by making a design statement on the walls or floor. Here, the busy look of dry brush strokes combines with the elegant simplicity of Japanese calligraphic characters. The result is a warm and uniquely stylish look that makes a memorable room.

## YOU WILL NEED

calligraphy brush

black ink

white paper

scissors

paper glue

foam block

craft knife

hammer

masking tape

emulsion paint: cream, rust and white

large and small paint rollers

dry paintbrush

ink: black and rust

matt varnish

**one** *Paint your Japanese characters with the calligraphy brush first, following the examples shown in this project. Make photocopies of each design. Cut the characters out roughly and glue one of each character to the foam. Keeping the knife at an angle, cut away all the white paper and the foam underneath it, to make a raised stamp.*

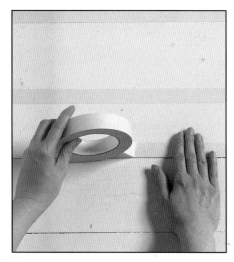

**two** *Prepare the floor, hammering in any protruding nails. Ensure it is clean and dry. Mask off both edges of alternate boards. Apply a base coat of cream emulsion and allow to dry.*

**three** *Draw a dry brush, dipped into a little neat rust paint, across the unmasked boards in a series of parallel strokes, allowing the base coat to show through in places. Repeat this exercise with white paint, which softens the whole effect. Leave to dry, then repeat the procedure with both colours on the remaining boards.*

**four** *Plan your design of Japanese characters, using spare photocopies of the characters, roughly cut out. Using a small roller, ink some of the stamps with black ink. Replace some of the photocopies with black stamped characters.*

**five** *Repeat, using the rust-coloured ink. Seal well with matt varnish and allow to dry.*

# CHINESE LANTERN

THIS STICK-AND-CARDBOARD lampshade has a natural look by day, but lights up like a skyscraper at night. Sheets of corrugated card can be bought in a range of colours, from natural to fluorescent, and the wooden skewers can also be painted. You can use the lantern over any small table lamp or even a candle. If using a candle, place it in a secure holder.

## YOU WILL NEED

metal ruler, approximately 3cm (1¼in) wide

pen or pencil

35 x 26cm (13¾ x 10¼in) sheet of corrugated card

cutting mat

scalpel

scrap paper

gold spray paint

packet of wooden skewers

**one** *Use the width of the ruler as a spacer and draw vertical lines across the cardboard's length. Cut slits across alternate columns, starting one in from the edge. Move the ruler down a width at a time; continue cutting to the bottom of the card.*

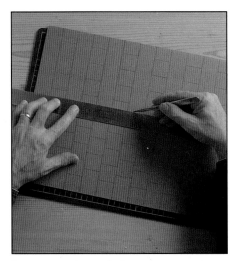

**two** *Cut through the uncut rows in the same way, but starting with the ruler a half-drop down, so that the slits fall halfway between the first ones. Continue until the sheet is covered with a "brickwork" pattern of slits.*

**three** *Protect your work surface with scrap paper, then spray the smooth side of the card with gold paint. Turn the card over and weave the skewers in and out of the slits. Allow about 2.5cm (1in) to protrude on one edge to give the shade legs to stand on. Trim the last column to within 1cm (½in) of the slits so that the join will not be too bulky. Overlapping the two edges (with the gold side inside), weave the last skewer through the double thickness to join the lampshade edges together.*

# HALF-TESTER

THIS POSITIVELY REGAL HALF-TESTER, draped with cool white cotton, will add majestic splendour to your bedroom. This sort of bed was popular around the second half of the nineteenth century, when fully-draped four-posters became less fashionable. The style imitates the ornate four-poster but is actually a box made to fit against the wall with a canopy that extends no more than a third of the length of the bed. This half-tester is made out of a batten and picture-frame moulding and adorned with plaster scrolls bought from a DIY store. The wall plaque is not strictly a part of the half-tester, but it adds the finishing touch. Use a fine white fabric, such as voile, muslin or cotton sheeting, for the drapes.

## YOU WILL NEED

plaster-cast head wall hanging

backing paper

shellac

paintbrushes

gold spray paint

black emulsion or poster paint

cloth

wire wool

2 scrolled plaster decorations

larger scrolled plaster decoration

155cm (62in) fancy picture-frame moulding

wood stain (optional)

5 x 2.5cm (2 x 1in) batten, 115cm (46in) long

155cm (62in) door-frame moulding

saw

mitring block

glue gun and glue sticks

1cm (¾in) wooden dowelling, 10cm (4in) long

curtain rings with clips

heavy-duty staple gun or eyelet screws

at least 10m (11yd) fine white fabric

scissors

drill, with appropriate drill bit

wall plugs

screwdriver and long screws

**one** *Place the plaster-cast head on a piece of backing paper to protect your work surface. Apply a coat of shellac to seal the surface. Allow the first coat to dry (for about 20 minutes), then apply a second coat of shellac. Allow to dry.*

**two** *Spray the head with gold spray paint. Allow to dry. Paint over the gold with black emulsion or poster paint. Cover the gold completely.*

**three** *Before the paint dries, rub most of it off using a slightly damp cloth. The black will have dulled the brassiness of the gold beneath.*

**four** *Burnish the high spots, such as the cheek bones, nose and brows, using wire wool. Give the scrolled decorations and picture-frame moulding the same treatment, or stain them with your chosen colour of wood stain. Cut the batten into one 75cm (30in) and one 40cm (16in) length. Cut the door-frame and picture-frame mouldings into one 75cm (30in) and two 40cm (16in) lengths.*

**five** *Using a mitring block, saw the corners on the door-frame and picture-frame mouldings that are to meet to make up the box shape. These will be both ends of the longest pieces and one end of each of the shorter ones.*

**six** *Glue the mitred door mouldings at the edges and fit the box shape together, placing the longest batten at the back. Surround the front three sides with the fancy moulding. Then glue the short batten in the centre of the piece as a reinforcement.*

**seven** *Cut the dowelling into two 5cm (2in) lengths and glue one piece into each top corner of the half-tester at the back of the moulding. They will act as supports for the scrolls.*

CONTINUED OVER ➤

**eight** *Apply hot glue to each length of dowelling, and then stick the corner scroll decorations in place.*

**nine** *Fix the curtain rings with clips at equal distances around the inside of the mouldings, using a heavy-duty staple gun or eyelet screws.*

**ten** *Cut the fabric in half along its length. Before putting up the half-tester, clip one length of fabric around one side to see how much fabric falls between each pair of clips. It will be easier to hang the drapes once the half-tester is in place if you have worked out the spacing in advance. Remove the fabric. Fix the half-tester to the wall near the ceiling, using appropriate fixings, and fix the plaster head to the wall. Clip the drapes in place and drape the fabric around the bed.*

# GILDED CHAIR

MANY A BEAUTIFUL BENTWOOD chair is relegated to the attic because its cane seat is damaged. Re-caning is expensive and it is hard to find skilled craftsmen; it often seems easier and cheaper to buy a new chair. This is a shame because a bentwood chair can become the star of a room, with some effort but little expense, by setting in a solid seat. Once the cane has been removed, the chair looks wonderful with gold-leaf decoration.

## YOU WILL NEED
wooden chair
craft knife
small screwdriver or bradawl
4 wooden blocks
pencil
saw
drill, with wood bit
8 wood screws
screwdriver
sheet of paper
scissors
sheet of plywood
masking tape
jigsaw (optional)
medium-grade sandpaper
size
paintbrush
gold leaf or 2 x 25-sheet packets of gold Dutch metal
clean, dry paintbrush
clean, dry cloth
varnish

**one** *If the seat needs repairing, cut away the cane with a craft knife and pick out the remaining strands with a screwdriver or bradawl. To make the supporting corner blocks, hold the pieces of wood inside each corner, mark the shape on the wood and then cut the pieces to shape. Hold a corner block in position and drill through it into the chair. Screw the block into position. Repeat for all four corners.*

**two** *Lay the paper over the seat and trace the shape. Cut out to create the template. Tape the template to the plywood and draw around it.*

**three** *Cut around the pencil line. (A timber merchant can do this for you if you do not have a jigsaw.) Sand the edges of the wooden seat to fit and drop it into place. Prepare the chair for gilding by sanding all the surfaces lightly. Roughening the wood helps the size to adhere.*

**four** *Paint the chair with size and allow it to dry. Follow the manufacturer's recommendations. Holding the gold leaf by the backing paper, lay a sheet on the chair. With a clean, dry brush, rub the gold leaf on to the chair. Continue until the chair is covered. It is very important that both the brush and your hands are clean and dry.*

**five** *Rub the chair with a clean, dry cloth to remove any loose flakes. Finally, to protect the gold leaf, seal the whole chair with varnish.*

# GUSTAVIAN CHAIR

PRETTY GUSTAVIAN PAINTED CHAIRS give a lightness and elegance to bedroom furniture. They are expensive because few are available outside Scandinavia, where they originated. Create your own by painting a wooden chair of classic shape. It should have a padded seat, pretty outlines and enough space on the back rest for a motif. Traditional colours are greys, dark blues, aquamarine, honey yellow and red, as well as white.

## YOU WILL NEED

classic wooden chair

medium- and fine-grade sandpaper

emulsion paint: white, blue and black

household paintbrush

fine and medium paintbrushes

monogram motif

tracing paper

soft and hard pencils

masking tape

clear matt varnish

typeface or script samples (e.g. from a calligraphy book)

large sheet of paper

scissors

1m (1yd) of 137cm (54in) (or twice seat-cover width) white cotton fabric

indelible laundry or fabric marker

staple gun

needle

matching thread

gold and silver spray paint

**one** *Lightly sand the chair with medium-grade sandpaper to make a key for the paintwork. Paint the chair with an undercoat of white emulsion. Mix blue-grey emulsion then, using the fine paintbrush, carefully outline the shape of the back of the chair. Add similar detailing to the seat and legs. Leave to dry. Trace your chosen letters and scrolls. Turn the tracing paper over, and rub all over the back with the soft pencil. Turn it over, position it on the chair back and tape it in place. Go over the outlines with a hard pencil to transfer them to the chair.*

**two** *Fill in the outlines in blue-grey with the medium paintbrush. Refer to your original reference for where the brush strokes should be thicker.*

**three** *Allow to dry. Apply a coat of matt varnish (water-based varnishes have very short drying times). Cut a piece of paper roughly the size of the chair seat pad, to give you an idea of the area to which you need to apply lettering. Photocopy type alphabets or sections of script, enlarging them, if necessary.*

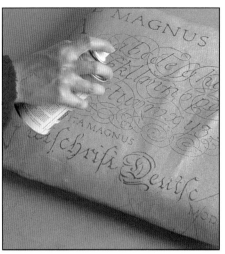

**four** *Cut up the script and arrange the pieces on the paper. Put the paper against a brightly lit window, and smooth the fabric over the design. Fix to the glass with masking tape. Using the fabric marker, carefully trace over the letters. Cover the seat pad with the fabric, securing it on the back with staples. Take a second piece of fabric, just smaller than the underside of the seat, turn under the edges and sew in place to cover the staples.*

**five** *Lightly spray over the whole seat with gold paint. Repeat with silver. Replace the seat pad in the chair. Lightly sand the paint with fine-grade sandpaper to give it a charming, slightly aged effect.*

# COPYCATS

CREATE A TRULY BEAUTIFUL setting by mixing fine, snowy-white linens, soft, filmy voile and crunchy tissue paper with gold lettering and initials. It looks extremely impressive and, although quite time-consuming, is easy to execute. Use any kind of calligraphy that appeals to you. (Here, the frontispiece from some sheet music was used.) Photocopy and enlarge your choice and trace it on to the voile, linen and tissue paper.

## YOU WILL NEED

typeface or script samples (e.g. from a calligraphy book)

voile for curtain

masking tape

gold fabric paint

fine paintbrushes

iron

tissue paper

gold acrylic paint

organza ribbon

linen hand towel

carbon paper or soft pencil (optional)

hard pencil (optional)

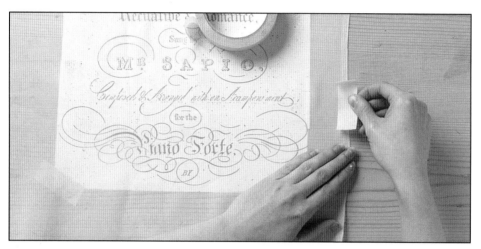

**one** *Select different types of script samples. You may not find everything you need from one source, so look out for individual details. Photocopy the script samples, enlarging them to size. Experiment by moving the pieces of script around to create pleasing combinations and arrangements. Position the photocopies on the voile for the curtain, devising a pattern along its length.*

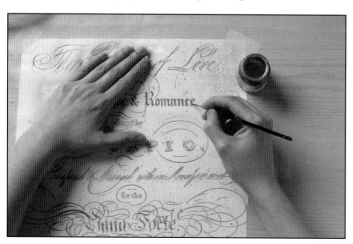

**two** *Tape your photocopy to a table or work surface, ensuring it is flat. Tape the fabric on top, so you can see the script through it. Using gold fabric paint and a fine paintbrush, trace the lettering on to the voile. Press the fabric, following the manufacturer's instructions, to set the colour.*

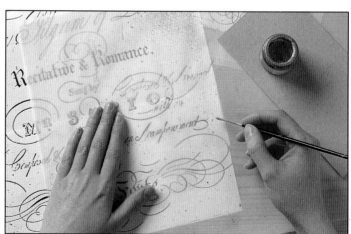

**three** *To decorate wrapping paper, trace different types of writing on to tissue paper, using gold acrylic paint. Complement the wrapping paper with a bow of white or gold-trimmed organza ribbon.*

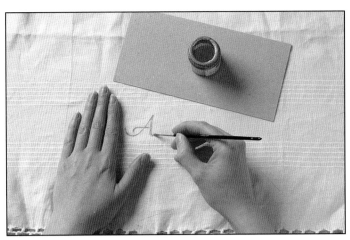

**four** *For the monogrammed hand towel, use paper cut-outs to plan your design. Tape the chosen letter flat on to a work surface. Lay the towel over the alphabet, and tape flat. Trace over the letter on to the towel with the fabric paint.*

**five** *If you wish to apply an initial to a chair or other piece of furniture, put carbon paper on to the back of the photocopied lettering or rub all over the back with a soft pencil. Then transfer this to the furniture by going over the outline with a harder pencil. Paint over the outline and leave to dry.*

# INDIAN SUMMER

THIS WINDOW SEAT RECESS was given a touch of glamorous Eastern mystery by layering fine, silky sari lengths behind each other to build up to a gloriously rich colour. The sunlight picks up the gold embroidered flecks and braids, and the star lantern between the curtains casts its own magic spell. If you have never been in a sari shop, you will be amazed by the vast range of exquisitely patterned silks and voiles you can buy.

## YOU WILL NEED

7 red and yellow sari lengths (or fewer)

braid, 7 metres (7 yd) plus width of each sari for braid edging

iron-on hem fix (such as Wundaweb)

iron

needle

matching sewing thread

wooden curtain rail

drill

wall plugs and hooks

wrought-iron curtain rail

**one** *If the saris do not have braid edges, add them with iron-on hem fix. Cut the remaining braid into 14cm (5½in) lengths to make seven loops for each sari. Space them at equal distances along the tops, and slip stitch. Put the wooden curtain rail through all the loops of three saris and fix it into the recess with hooks. Hang the iron rail on the outer frame, and hang two saris on the left by threading their loops alternately so that one hangs in front. Hang the two other saris on the right.*

**two** *Separate the red and yellow saris, holding one in each hand about halfway down their length.*

**three** *Wrap the yellow one round the red one and knot them together. Arrange the folds of the knot so that the fabric tumbles away and spills to the floor.*

# INDIAN TEMPLE BEDHEAD

INDIAN TEMPLE WALL PAINTINGS are the inspiration for this arch-shaped bedhead. The bedroom feels as if it has been magically transported thousands of miles, but the real magic here comes in a simple pot of paint. Before painting the bedhead, set the mood with a deep rust-coloured wash on the walls. If you can, use a water-based distemper for an authentic powdery bloom. If you are using emulsion, thin it with water.

## YOU WILL NEED

large roll of brown parcel wrap

felt-tipped pen

masking tape (optional)

scissors

spray adhesive

chalk

water-based paint: dark blue, bright blue and red

plate

kitchen sponge

sandy cream emulsion paint

medium and fine paintbrushes

fine-grade sandpaper

**one** *Refer to the diagram on the right that shows the shape of the arch. Transfer a half-arch on to brown parcel wrap, enlarging it as required using a grid system. Alternatively, tape a sheet of brown parcel wrap on the wall and draw the half-arch directly on to it, following the pattern shape.*

**two** *Cut out the half-arch shape, using a pair of scissors. Position the paper pattern on the wall with spray adhesive and draw around the edges with chalk.*

**three** *Flip the pattern and draw around it to produce the second half of the arch. Spread some dark blue paint on to a plate and use a damp sponge to dab it on to the central panel. Don't cover the background completely, but leave some of the wall colour showing through. When the paint is dry, apply the bright blue paint over the dark blue in the same way.*

**four** *When the paint is dry, paint the arch in sandy cream emulsion, using a medium-sized paintbrush. When the emulsion paint is dry, rub it back in places with fine-grade sandpaper to give a faded effect. Outline the inside and outside of the arch with the red paint, using a fine paintbrush. Support your painting hand with your free hand and use the width of the brush to make a single line. Outline the outer red stripe with a thinner dark blue line.*

**five** *Leave to dry, then use fine-grade sandpaper to soften any hard edges and give the arch the naturally faded appearance of an old temple wall.*

# PISTACHIO-SHELL BORDER

IN INDIA THE DECORATION on floors and walls is as varied as the materials available. The floors of temples and shrines are often intricately patterned with natural objects, such as seeds, shells and stones. Restrict your decoration to places where you don't normally wear shoes. You can fill in just a small area or a whole border. A corner about 1.2 x 1.2m (4 x 4 ft) takes about 3kg (7lb) of unshelled pistachio nuts.

## YOU WILL NEED
cream emulsion paint
paint roller
paint-mixing tray
ruler
pencil
masking tape
blue acrylic eggshell paint
paintbrushes
PVA glue
pistachio shells
natural sponge
eggshell emulsion paint:
peach, cream and pale blue

**one** *Make sure your floor surface is sound, dry and level; cover with hardboard or marine-plywood if necessary. Apply a base coat of cream emulsion. Measure and draw out your straight borders and edge them with masking tape. Draw your curved shapes straight on to the floor free-hand or using a traced shape. Fill in the lines with blue paint.*

**two** *Apply plenty of thick PVA glue to a small blue area. Apply the shells, working on the fine areas first. You may find you need to grade the shells by size, in advance.*

**three** *When the PVA is dry, paint blue over the shells and touch up any cream areas that need it. Randomly sponge the area inside the border, with the darkest colour first.*

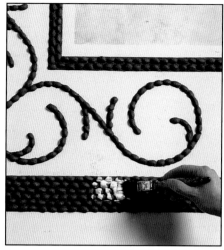

**four** *Allow to dry completely and then repeat, using a softer shade of the same colour (in the photograph, peach mixed with cream). Allow to dry and then use the same technique to apply a new colour (in the photograph, pale blue) over it.*

**five** *Seal the floor with watered-down PVA, as recommended by the manufacturer; it should be applied thickly over the shells. The whiteness will disappear as it dries, leaving a clear surface. Allow to dry completely.*

# FILIGREE WOODEN PANEL

RADIATOR PANELLING NEED not be used only for its original purpose; it can also be used to create an unusual wall covering. It often comes in a variety of interesting designs that make it worth using over a much larger area. Turn it on its side and attach it above a skirting board to bring it up to dado-rail height. When choosing the colours bear in mind that the background must be strong enough to show through the panelling.

### YOU WILL NEED
scrap paper
pencil
ruler
radiator panelling
white chinagraph pencil
jig-saw or hack-saw
emulsion paint in 2 colours
paintbrushes
paint roller
paint-mixing tray
spirit level
straight edge
drill, with masonry and wood bits
wall plugs
hammer
wood screws
glue gun and glue sticks

**one** *Plan the pattern on paper and decide where cuts in the radiator panelling are necessary. Mark off the sections to be cut out with a chinagraph pencil. Use a jig-saw or hack-saw to remove them. Choose the colour.*

**two** *Paint the wall and leave to dry. Meanwhile, paint the panelling. Using a spirit level and straight edge, mark a horizontal guideline for attaching the panelling to the wall.*

**three** *Drill holes in the wall for the panelling. Hammer wall plugs into the holes. Drill holes in the panelling to correspond with the wall plugs. Screw the panelling in position on the wall. Glue the panelling to the wall here and there, with the glue gun, to hold it flat against the wall. Then attach the border above. You can place a dado rail between the two, if you wish.*

# TEXTURED GOLD FLOOR

EXOTIC SOUVENIRS FROM far-flung places sometimes require a dramatic backdrop to set them off. Gold and copper are suitably flamboyant, but texture is also needed. Builders' scrim, used to reinforce plaster, fits the bill. It gives a surface that traps different amounts of gold and copper, creating the effect of beaten metal. As with all exotic finishes, the delight is more in the instant transformation than in practicality.

## YOU WILL NEED
tape measure
pencil
paper
ruler
power sander, with fine-grade sandpaper
builders' scrim
scissors
PVA glue
oil-based gold paint
wide paintbrush
copper powder paint
heavy-duty floor varnish

**one** *Measure the floor. Take into account the width of the scrim, plan your design on paper first to make sure that your pattern doesn't leave awkward half lines at the edges. You may need to lay marine-plywood or hardboard to ensure a smooth, flat surface. Lightly sand the floor to make sure it's perfectly flat.*

**two** *Cut the lengths of scrim, starting with the longest, and lay it to your pattern. Conceal joins where two lengths cross underneath, overlapping the ends by at least 15cm (6in).*

**three** *Stick the scrim down with PVA glue. Brush out any glue that soaks through to the top to hold the scrim firmly. Don't worry if you spread glue outside the area of the scrim. Pencil in a few guidelines and put a weight on the other end of the scrim to keep it straight.*

**four** *Dilute the PVA with water and coat the whole floor, going over the stuck-down scrim as well. This seals the floor and forms a key for the paint.*

**five** *Paint on the gold paint with the wide brush, covering the whole floor. If using an oil-based paint, ensure you have plenty of ventilation in the room. Allow to dry. Dust the copper powder paint over the scrim, allowing it to be trapped by the mesh surface. Apply at least two coats of heavy-duty floor varnish to seal.*

# $\mathscr{A}$MERICAN DREAM

LIE IN STATE EVERY NIGHT, draped in the Stars and Stripes of America or any brightly coloured flag that takes your fancy. This is a great bed-covering idea and different rooms can have different flags to complement different colour schemes. The timber-clad walls and peg-rail above the bed give the room a ranch-house feel that looks great alongside brilliant red, white and blue.

### YOU WILL NEED
2 large flags
pillow
packet of safety pins
wooden buttons
needle and thread
quilt

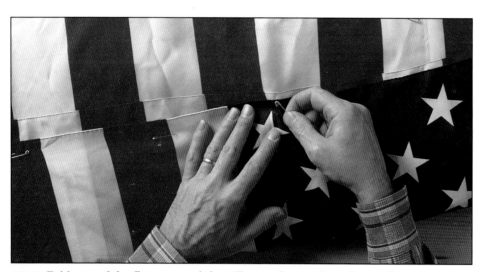

**one** *Fold one of the flags around the pillow and use safety pins to close the long seam.*

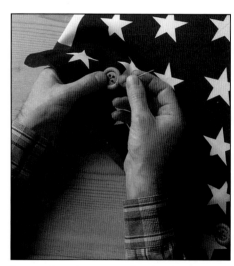

**two** *Sew three wooden buttons along one pillow edge to hold the seam closed. Leave the other edge open so the pillow can be removed.*

**three** *Select an assortment of wooden buttons to attach around the edge and across the centre of the second flag.*

**four** *Lay the flag over the quilt. Sew on the buttons, stitching through both the flag and the quilt, so that the layers are held together.*

# SHELL SHOCKED

AFTER HOLIDAYING, MAKE your shell collection into something really special. We have used them to decorate fine voile curtains, and added interest with eyelets along the top threaded with string loops. On this theme, an easy, effective way of trimming a wall is with a length of fine rope attached at dado-rail height. Fix a row of tiny shells above. To complete the look, paint a terracotta pot white and attach a small sand dollar to the front.

## YOU WILL NEED

iron-on interfacing (optional)

tape measure

dressmaker's scissors

cotton voile, the required drop, plus 4 x the window width

dressmaker's pins

needle and tacking thread

sewing machine

matching sewing thread

chrome eyelets

hammer

wooden block

rough natural string

glue gun and glue sticks

electric drill, with very fine drill bit (optional)

fine beading wire

beading needle (optional)

terracotta pot

matt white emulsion paint

paintbrush

sand dollar shell

**one** *To give extra body to the headings of fine fabrics, cut a length of iron-on interfacing 5 cm (2 in) wide and bond it to the wrong side of the voile. Pin, tack, press and machine-stitch the heading across the top and the hem at the bottom. Then turn under a 1cm (½in) hem down each side. Pin, tack, press and sew. Mark the positions of the eyelets with pins.*

**two** *Fix the eyelets, following the manufacturer's instructions. Find a secure surface when hammering the eyelets in place.*

**three** *Cut equal lengths of string, thread the strings through the eyelets and knot the ends. Cut lengths of wire and use a glue gun to stick them on to the shells. Alternatively, drill holes in the shells. A combination of these methods may be helpful, depending on the shape of the shells. Position the shells on the curtains.*

**four** *Use the beading wire to "sew" the shells on to the curtain by hand, as invisibly as possible.*

**five** *Paint the terracotta pot white. Put a little glue on the side of the pot and attach the sand dollar.*

# SHEER MAGIC

TRIM A PLAIN LINEN or hessian bed cover and pillowcase with the sheerest of voile fabrics to give a look that is simple, tailored and elegant. Large bone buttons and the rougher textures of hessian and linen are the perfect foil to the fineness of the fabric. Cut the voile slightly longer than the drop on the bed so it falls on to the floor all around. The amount of voile given here is for a double bed, but the idea can be adapted to suit any bed size.

## YOU WILL NEED

tape measure

about 7m (7½yds) cotton voile

dressmaker's scissors

dressmaker's pins

needle

tacking thread

sewing machine

matching sewing thread

hessian or fine linen bed cover

16 large bone buttons

fine embroidery scissors

tapestry needle

fine string

pillow

**one** *For the top of the cover, you will need a piece of voile the length of the bed plus the drop on one end. The piece should be 15cm (6in) narrower than the width of the bed so the buttons will not be too near the edge. Allow 10cm (4in) all round for double hems. For the sides, you will need two pieces the length of the bed. Measure the drop from the buttons to the floor, allowing 10cm (4 in) for hems as before. Pin, tack and sew all the hems.*

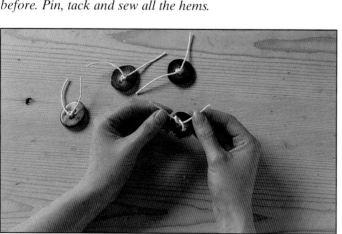

**two** *Mark the position of the buttons and buttonholes. They must correspond exactly. Sew the buttonholes then cut the centres carefully. Use a tapestry needle and fine string to sew the buttons in position on the hessian bed cover, and button the voile cover on top.*

**three** *For the pillowcase, cut a piece of hessian the depth of the pillow and twice the length, plus seam allowances on the long sides. With right sides together, pin, tack and sew the top and bottom edges. Turn right-side out and press.*

**four** *To make a fringed edge, find a thread running across the pillow, just in from the cut edge. Pull gently to fray the edge. Use the same method to make an over-cover for the pillow from voile. Hem all the edges.*

**five** *Mark the position of the button-holes in each corner. Machine-stitch the button-holes and cut the centres. Sew buttons on to the corners of the hessian pillow cover, and button the voile cover over the top.*

# CALICO TENT

GET THAT HOLIDAY FEELING every morning when you look out on the day from your tent. This could make a novelty bedhead for a child's bedroom or a stylish feature in a adult's bedroom. The tent is made using a combination of fittings intended for different purposes. The chrome rods are shower rails, finished off in copper with plumber's pipe caps. The thin copper tube is also from the plumbing department – it has an attractive finish and can be bent easily with long-nosed pliers. The stability of the tent is assured by the use of shower rail sockets on the wall and a line of cup hooks on the ceiling. The fabric used here is unbleached calico.

## YOU WILL NEED

8 x 1m (8¾ x 1yd) unbleached calico

tape measure

pencil and ruler

scissors

6m (6½yds) iron-on hemming tape

iron

hacksaw

150cm (60in) length of chrome shower rail

centre punch

hammer

drill, with bit (the size of the copper tube)

1m (1yd) narrow copper tube

long-nosed pliers

3 chrome shower rail sockets

spirit level

screwdriver

6 chrome cup hooks and wall plugs

4m (4½yds) white cord

3 copper pipe caps (to fit shower rail)

**one** *Decide on the height of the top of the tent. Measure off the fabric and tear it to size. Fold the fabric in four to find the centre and mark this point. Measure 36cm (14in) down each short edge and mark the points.*

**two** *Draw a connecting line between the centre point and each of the side points to give the shape for the top.*

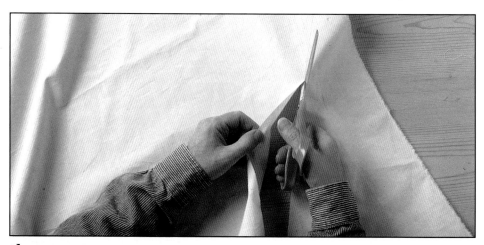

**three** *Cut along the drawn lines, then cut a 3cm (1¼in) notch at each of the points of the tent shape. Fold the fabric over to make a 3cm (1¼in) seam around the top and sides of the fabric.*

**four** *Use iron-on hemming tape to hold down the seams neatly. The two pieces should now meet at a right angle to make the tent shape. The sides and top of the tent will fold back to give a double thickness of fabric. Make three holes for the rails at the corner points and reinforce the fabric with an extra square of calico ironed on with hemming tape.*

**five** *Use a hack-saw to cut the length of chrome shower rail into three 50cm (20in) pieces.*

**six** *Use a centre punch to dent the shower rail where the holes will be drilled, so that the drill does not slip. You will need to drill a hole 5cm (2in) from one end of two of the poles and two holes in the other pole, the first 5cm (2in) from one end and the second 1cm (½in) in from it.*

**seven** *Drill the holes using a drill bit the same size as the copper tube. Use a hacksaw to cut two lengths of copper tube. Use the long-nosed pliers to bend one end of each copper tube into a hook shape. Use the chrome rail to estimate the curve of the hooks. Each hook should fit snugly around the chrome rail with its end fitting into the drilled hole.*

**eight** *Position the shower rail sockets on the wall so that the rails slot into them. Use a spirit level to check that the outer two are level.*

CONTINUED OVER ➤

*Above: The hooked copper tubes fit over and into the chrome rail. The cord is looped around the rail and crossed over to suspend the tent front from the cup hooks. The side rail is finished off with the copper cap and suspended from a crossed cord attached to the cup hooks.*

**nine** *Refer to the diagram below. Push the chrome rails through the holes in the back of the tent, then fit the copper tubes in place to hold the front section rigid. Fit the straight end of each copper tube into the hole in each side rail. Fit the hooked ends over the middle rail and into the two drilled holes. Fix a row of cup hooks to the ceiling directly above the front edge of the tent. Loop white cord around the cup hooks and the chrome rails for added stability. Finally, cap the chrome pipes with the copper caps.*

# $\mathcal{J}$EASIDE SETTING

SOOTHE THE SOUL AND mind by strolling along the beach and at the same time, searching the shoreline for all kinds of wonderful things: strands of seaweed, pieces of driftwood, soft grey pebbles, birds' feathers, pearly sea shells and chalky white stones with holes ready-made for threading them on to pieces of twine. Make the most of your natural treasures by using them to decorate mirrors, picture frames and trinket boxes, or any other unadorned objects – their uses are endless. Sea shells also make wonderfully evocative candle holders.

## YOU WILL NEED

**DRIFTWOOD AND PEBBLE FRAMES**
distressed-wood frames
PVA glue (optional)
medium-grade sandpaper
wood stain and paintbrush (optional)
about 50cm (20in) thick rope
staple gun or hammer and tacks
driftwood
glue gun and glue sticks
seaweed
pebbles and stones
sea shells

**PEBBLE AND STONE NECKLACES**
raffia
tiny pebbles
smooth coloured glass
glue gun and glue sticks

**SHELL CANDLEHOLDERS**
burnt-down candles
kitchen knife
sea shells
safety matches

**one** *For the driftwood frame, re-glue the joints, if necessary. Sand it along the grain and stain it, if you wish. To hang the mirror, attach the rope to the top of the frame, with a staple gun or hammer and tacks. Arrange the driftwood pieces around the frame. Experiment with different positions until you are happy with the result.*

**two** *Use a glue gun to fix the driftwood in place, making sure the pieces are perfectly secure.*

**three** *Work out the position of the seaweed so it drapes gently across the mirror. Add the pebbles, stones and shells, raising them slightly off the edge so they are reflected in the mirror. Glue the pebbles and other materials in place.*

**four** *For the pebble frame, use a similar frame base to the driftwood frame and sand and stain as before, if required. Select a pleasing variety of stones. Arrange them to your liking and glue them on the frame.*

**five** *For the pebble and stone necklace, tie a length of raffia around tiny stones and pieces of smooth coloured glass. Use a glue gun to apply a tiny dot of glue to each knot where the stone or glass is tied. For the candles in shells, cut the candles right down with a knife and stand them in a shell. Light the candles and allow the wax to drip down until it fills the shells. Blow out the flame. The wax then solidifies to the shape of the shell.*

# BUTTERFLY MONTAGE

SURREALISM AND THE WORK of artists such as Ernst, Escher, and Magritte inspire surprising ways of depicting unusual yet familiar objects in designs for montages. This butterfly floor could easily have been made using motifs of flowers, boats or chairs. Strong lines are important, and there are books of wonderful line drawings available. Lay the motifs down in an ordered pattern. Here the design suggests the flight of butterflies. Protect the montage from wear and tear, by applying half a dozen coats of varnish.

## YOU WILL NEED
light-coloured emulsion paint
paintbrushes
motifs
craft knife
self-healing cutting mat
wallpaper paste
indelible felt-tipped pen or fine artist's brush and oil-based paints
matt varnish

**one** *Make sure your floor is completely smooth. If necessary, lay a hardboard or marine-plywood floor. Paint the floor a light colour so that the motifs will show up. Photocopy your chosen image(s) in at least seven sizes, ranging from quite small to fairly large.*

**two** *Using a craft knife and a cutting mat, carefully cut out every image.*

**three** *Decide on the positions of your images and stick them in place with wallpaper paste.*

**four** *Add remaining fine details with a fine artist's brush and/or an indelible felt-tipped pen. Finish by applying at least six coats of varnish to be sure of its durability (some acrylic varnishes dry very quickly) or apply a very strong floor varnish.*

# BILLOWING MUSLIN

FLOATY BUTTER MUSLIN IS one of the cheapest ways to cover a large window without blocking out all the light. The muslin here is in two pieces, each long enough to drape over the rail and down to the floor on both sides. One of the lengths was stamped with a sponge cut-out in the shape of a melon half. The two pieces were hung next to each other and knotted about halfway down so the stamped half crosses over to the other side.

## YOU WILL NEED

tracing paper

pencil

thin card, for template

block of high-density foam (the type used for camping mattresses)

craft knife

2 lengths of butter muslin

2 bamboo poles, window width

sewing machine (optional)

needle

matching sewing thread

fabric paint: coffee-brown and dark brown

plate

paint roller or brush

tape

drill, and masonry bit

wall plugs and cup hooks

bundle of natural-coloured raffia

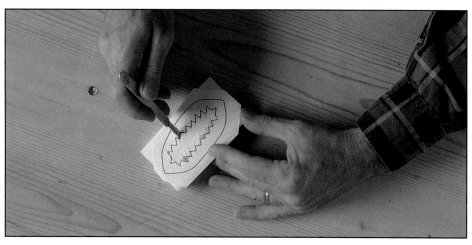

**one** *Trace the template, enlarging to the required size. Place it on the foam block, then cut around it. Scoop out the inner area, leaving the printing surface intact. Fold both of the muslin lengths in half. Form a channel along the top of each, about 5cm (2in) down from the fold. It must be the width of the two bamboo poles, as they will slide into it. Sew by machine or hand.*

**two** *Put some of the coffee-brown fabric paint on to the plate and run the roller through it until it is thoroughly and evenly coated. Use the roller to ink the foam stamp.*

**three** *Start stamping the pattern, rotating the stamp in your hand each time you print. Leave more or less the same amount of space between prints.*

**four** *Stamp darker prints randomly among lighter ones. Fix the fabric paint according to the manufacturer's instructions. Tape over the ends of the bamboo poles so that they do not catch on the muslin, and slide them through the sewn channels in the curtains.*

**five** *Drill holes and insert the wall plugs and cup hooks in the top of the window recess, about 10–15cm (4–6in) in from the sides. Cut ten 45cm (18in) strips of raffia and use five on either side, twisted together into a rope, to bind the bamboo poles together in place of the tape. Use the loose ends to suspend the bamboo rail by tying them to the cup hooks. Tie a knot with the two curtains about halfway down their length. Experiment with different effects, but take your time over the positioning of the knot, its shape and the way the muslin drapes over it.*

# CORRUGATED HEADBOARD

CORRUGATED CARDBOARD HAS been liberated from its role as a packaging material as designers realize its potential and versatility. It is strong, rigid, insulating, economical and light as a feather. This project celebrates the natural cardboard colour, but coloured sheets are also available and are great for adding decorative touches. Corrugated cardboard is perfect for experimentation, especially as it is so inexpensive.

## YOU WILL NEED

glue gun and glue sticks

5 x 2.5cm (2 x 1in) batten, to fit around the edges of the MDF

rectangle of MDF, to fit behind the bed

roll of corrugated cardboard 1m (1yd) high

set square

scissors

staple gun and staples

ruler

pencil

scalpel or craft knife

cutting mat or thick card

small rubber roller

**one** *Use the glue gun to stick the thin battens to the back of the MDF around the edges. This will be hidden, so any glue drips will not show. Place a large piece of corrugated cardboard over the front of the MDF. Use a set square to press against and crease the cardboard neatly for folding at the corners. Fold the cardboard neatly around the corners in the same way that you would wrap a parcel.*

**two** *Trim away any excess cardboard that may cause the corners to look bulky. Staple the flaps down, pressing the gun firmly against the cardboard from above to prevent any kickback that may cause the staples to protrude.*

**three** *Carefully staple the cardboard along the strips of wood, keeping it taut as you go along. Cut four strips of cardboard 7.5cm (3in) wide, and approximately 45cm (18in) long. Use the rubber roller to flatten down the ridges. Fold the strips into three along their length, so that they are 2.5cm (1in) wide. Again, use the rubber roller to flatten the strips.*

**four** *Position the strips to form a diamond shape in the centre of the headboard. Allow the ends to overlap each other. Staple the strips in place. Cut through the two overlapping layers with scissors to mitre the corners. Staple the strips as closely as possible to the mitred ends.*

**five** *For the spiral turrets, cut seven 50cm (20in) strips of cardboard. One long edge of each strip is cut at an angle: cut the first two strips along a line sloping from one short edge of 10cm (4in) to the other short edge of 5cm (2in). Cut the second two strips from one edge of 12cm (4¾in) to the other of 5cm (2in). Cut the next two from 14cm (5½in) to 5cm (2in). Cut the last strip from 16cm (6¼in) to 5cm(2in). Starting at the wider end, roll up the cardboard with the ridges on the outside. Keep the base straight. Use the glue gun to stick down the end of each turret. Arrange the turrets on top of the headboard so that the tallest one is in the middle. Stick them down using the hot-glue gun. Use plenty of glue in the middle and less towards the outside to achieve a good bond without any mess.*

# THE NEW WAVE

CORRUGATED PAPER IS A much-maligned material that can look absolutely stunning if used innovatively. It is easy to work with and has myriad uses. Experiment with different shapes to see which looks most pleasing. Triangles would look great bordering a door frame, for example, and perhaps following the lines of the skirting. Bear in mind that corrugated paper crushes very easily so, before starting work, flatten it with a ruler.

## YOU WILL NEED

tape measure

roll of natural corrugated paper

scissors

ruler

thin cardboard

pencil

craft knife

self-healing cutting mat

aerosol adhesive

masking tape (optional)

candles

white emulsion paint

paintbrush

glue gun and glue sticks

natural string

straight-sided vase

fine corrugated paper in different colours

paper glue

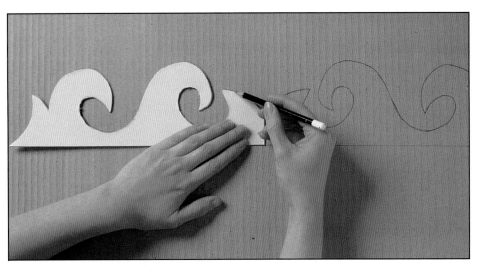

**one** *Measure the width of the sill and cut the corrugated paper to this measurement, plus the required drop. Flatten the ridges with a ruler. Draw the design on to cardboard and cut out a template. Draw the shape on the natural corrugated paper, using the template. Cut it out with a craft knife on a cutting mat.*

**two** *Spray the back of the corrugated paper with adhesive and fix in place. If you want to remove the decoration later, stick masking tape under the sill and glue the decoration to the tape.*

**three** *For the candle-wrappers, cut strips of corrugated paper to the right size and paint them with white emulsion. Slit the corrugations with scissors. Cut a wider strip and glue it to the back of the white strip. Wrap the decoration round the candles. Cut string long enough to wrap several times round the candles. Use the same technique to make a decoration for a straight-sided vase.*

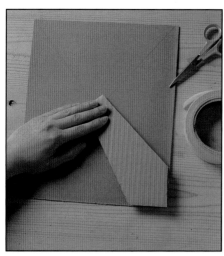

**four** *To make the picture frame, measure the image that will be framed and decide on the size and shape required. Draw the frame backing on to corrugated cardboard and cut it out with the craft knife and ruler. Use the backing as a template to draw and cut out the front of the frame from coloured corrugated paper. Cut out the central frame area. Stick the image in position with paper glue so the backing colour shows through in a thin border all round.*

**five** *Make a stand for the frame, with a piece of corrugated cardboard cut to the shape shown. Decorate the frame with twisted strips of coloured paper.*

# CORRUGATED LAMPBASE

CORRUGATED CARDBOARD HAS SCULPTURAL qualities that elevate it from a boring packaging material. Its construction, with one smooth and one rigid side, means that it can be rolled into even, tubular shapes to make a lamp base. This is one project in which the fact that corrugated cardboard is very lightweight might be a disadvantage, so take care to site the lamp where it is unlikely to be knocked over.

**one** *Cut a 52 x 35cm (20½ x 13¾in) rectangle of corrugated cardboard and roll it lengthways, leaving the centre hollow for the lamp fitting. Glue the loose edge.*

**two** *Cut a 135 x 4cm (53 x 1½in) rectangle from the corrugated cardboard. Measure in 18cm (7¼in) from the top-left corner, draw a line between this point and the bottom-right corner and cut along this line. Apply glue to the square end and line it up with the column base. Wrap it around, gluing to hold the layers together. Keep the base flat.*

**three** *Cut a 52 x 4cm (20½ x 1½in) rectangle of corrugated cardboard, then glue and wrap it around the base to add extra stability.*

**four** *Cut another 135 x 4cm (53 x 1½in) rectangle of corrugated cardboard, then glue and wrap this around the top of the column. Keep the top flat. Ask an electrician to install the bottle-adaptor lamp fitting and to wire it to a flex.*

# Novelty Rooms

THIS IS THE PERFECT place to let your imagination run riot, with customized designs for children — and adults. But if you plan to decorate a child's room, first ask the occupant. You may think Pooh Bear makes an excellent wall stencil, but younger heads may be thinking along the lines of not-so-cuddly extinct creatures...

Whatever you decide on should be regarded as temporary. The first rule of decorating a child's bedroom, for instance, is not to do anything that can't be changed easily. Tastes change and fads go as quickly as they arrive. Bearing this in mind, make everything as big, bright and bold as possible. You may not agree with the aesthetics of it all, but a room with a sense of humour is great fun — and a stimulating environment for children, especially if they feel able to let themselves go in it. That means not being too precious about the room. Everything should be as practical and hard-wearing as possible. Such a decorating challenge opens up endless opportunities. For the floor choose differently coloured carpet tiles arranged as for a board game. Kids like writing on walls, so let them — provide a wall-to-wall blackboard with a colourful border.

*Comic strips are recognized everywhere and a montage of well-known characters can be used for a brilliant decorative focal point in a teenager's bedroom.*

Laundry baskets topped by brightly coloured domes make great storage containers. Stencil the walls with flags which are colourful and easy to prepare, or simply turn a wall into a patchwork of colour. Our secret for getting the perfect finish is so easy the kids can do it. Grown-ups too will love these innovative ideas that transform a room in next to no time.

Budding astronauts will love the padded headboard covered with space blankets and you can make individual duvet covers for each child. Many of our ideas for stencilling and painting can be done by the children, so don't be backward in coming forward to ask for their help. Their street cred may depend on it!

# WALL BLACKBOARD

THIS SIMPLE BLACKBOARD is lots of fun as well as being a highly practical wall treatment for a child's bedroom or playroom. Make sure the wall is flat before you start, and paint it with undercoat and two coats of emulsion first, if necessary. Bear the height of the child in mind when you are deciding on the size and position of the blackboard. Blackboard paint is available from most good paint suppliers.

## YOU WILL NEED

tape measure

pencil

spirit level

straight edge

masking tape

blackboard paint

paintbrushes

emulsion paint in several colours

tracing paper (optional)

craft knife (optional)

self-healing cutting mat (optional)

stencil brush

hooks

string

chunky chalks

**one** *Measure and draw the blackboard and the border on the wall, using the spirit level and straight edge. Mask off the blackboard with tape and apply two coats of blackboard paint. Remove the masking tape immediately. Leave to dry.*

**two** *Mask off the border and paint with two coats of emulsion. Remove the masking tape immediately.*

**three** *Mask off the diamond shape or draw and cut a stencil from tracing paper, using the craft knife and cutting mat. Tape it to the wall. Paint the diamonds with a stencil brush. Paint the hooks. Screw them into the wall and attach the chalks.*

# FLAG STENCILS

**HERE'S A STRONG DESIGN** to add lively colour and an element of fun to a child's room, while avoiding the conventional and rather predictable motifs and colours available in ready-made children's wallpapers. The easiest way to make a unique stencil is to photocopy a simple motif on to acetate: here, two complementary flag motifs are combined. Use the stencils as a border at picture- or dado-rail height, randomly around the room or in straight lines to make a feature of, for example, a chimney breast on one wall or an alcove behind a desk or bookshelves.

## YOU WILL NEED

acetate sheet

craft knife

self-healing cutting mat

sticky tape

black emulsion paint

stencil brush or small paintbrush

emulsion paint in several bright colours

**one** *Photocopy the designs from the back of the book in various sizes to try them out. When you are happy with the size, photocopy them directly on to the acetate.*

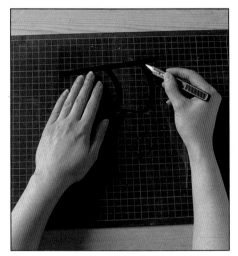

**two** *Cut out the stencils carefully, using a craft knife and cutting mat. Tape the stencil to the wall.*

**three** *Stencil a bold outline in black.*

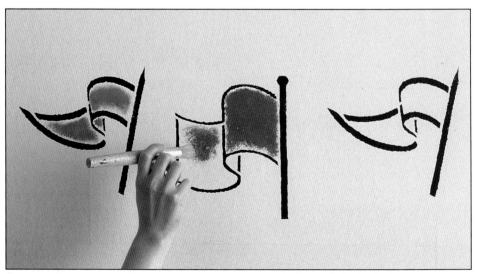

**four** *Use a stencil brush to apply colour inside the outline, or paint it free-hand for a looser, more appropriate effect for a child's room.*

# PURPLE PLAYROOM

THESE LUSH PURPLE FELT drapes knock the socks off most playroom curtains! They are inspired by the felt shapes that children play with. There is a wide range of topics available – from farms to fairies. When you press out the pre-cut shapes you get a great negative shape as well as your motif. The curtains are attached to a wooden batten, extending 20cm (8in) beyond the frame on both sides above the window.

## YOU WILL NEED

wooden batten, 5 x 2.5cm (2 x 1in) thick

spirit level

drill, and masonry bit

wall plugs and screws

screwdriver

pinking shears

deep purple felt, 2m (2yd) wide x the drop plus 40cm (16in)

commercial pre-cut felt shapes

fabric glue

chalk

drawing pins

staple gun (optional)

**one** *Fix the batten above the window extending at least 20cm (8in) beyond the frame on both sides. Use pinking shears to cut two strips of curtain felt the width of the curtain fabric and 2cm(¾in) deeper than the pre-cut felt squares. Stick the felt backgrounds along the strips with fabric glue, allowing space for the gathers.*

**two** *Stick the strips on the wrong side of the top edge of the curtains (i.e. the side that will not be decorated). On the right side of the curtain, draw a chalk line 40cm (16in) from the top. Pin the curtain edges to meet in the centre of the batten, holding the top 40cm (16in) above it. Pin the outside edges to each end of the batten.*

**three** *Pin or staple the curtains into pleats.If you use pins, you can adjust the pleats as you go. When the pleating is complete, allow the pelmet to flop down.*

**four** *Arrange all the felt shapes randomly on the curtains. They will cling for long enough for you to make a design you like. Stick the shapes in place with fabric glue.*

**five** *You can make tiebacks in the same style as the pelmet.*

# ℬEADED LAUNDRY BASKET

**BRIGHTLY COLOURED PLASTIC** laundry baskets are cheap and practical, but they need help to give them a more individual look. This purple laundry basket was made glamorous with bright Chinese checker pieces taken from an inexpensive children's set. They are ideal as the domed pieces have spiked backs that can be trimmed to the required depth and glued into holes drilled in the plastic. The fixing is very secure, so don't worry about beads scattering all over the bedroom floor! This decorated basket is not suitable for children under three, who might swallow the checker pieces and choke.

## YOU WILL NEED
Chinese checker pieces
wire cutters
plastic laundry basket with lid
drill, with fine bit
glue gun with all-purpose glue sticks (or all-purpose glue)
masking tape

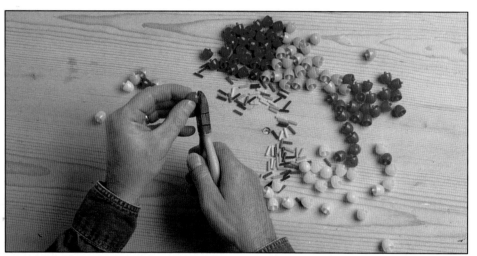

**one** *Sort the Chinese checker pieces into colours. Trim the spikes so that the pieces will fit into the depth of the plastic basket without protruding on the other side.*

**two** *Drill holes for the spikes – a circle on the lid and lines down the sides.*

**three** *Sort the pieces into the colour sequence you want. Apply glue to one spike at a time and push it into a hole. The glue sets quickly, so work fast.*

**four** *Run a length of masking tape round the base of the basket as a positioning guide for a straight band of coloured pieces. Fix these as you did the other pieces.*

# CHILD'S BEDROOM NOOK

YOUNG CHILDREN LIKE THE security of enclosed sleeping spaces, and older children relish the privacy, especially if the room is shared with a brother or sister. In this project, MDF panels are positioned around an existing bed. They can be attached to the bed base or simply rested in a corner so that they enclose the space but cannot be pushed over. The stencils used to decorate the MDF panels and the bed linen can also be used on the walls.

## YOU WILL NEED

2 sheets MDF, 122cm (48in) x width of the bed

1 sheet MDF, 122cm (48in) x length of the bed, plus 5cm (2in)

5 x 2.5cm (2 x 1in) baton, 122cm (48in) long

drill, with size 10 bit

screwdriver and suitable screw fixings

pale grey emulsion paint

paintbrush

paper

spray adhesive

stencil card

scalpel or craft knife

cutting mat or thick card

white pillowcase

iron

masking tape

fabric paint: red, blue and yellow

plate

stencil brushes

white sheet or duvet cover

soft and hard pencils

jigsaw

fine-grade sandpaper

stencil paints (optional)

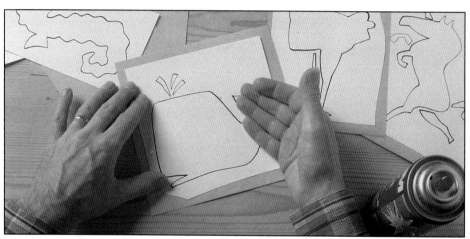

**one** *The shorter pieces of MDF are used for the head and foot of the bed. To make the bed surround, screw the baton to butt up to one 122cm (48in) edge of the head and foot pieces. Butt the long piece of MDF at right angles against the baton on the bedhead and screw in place. Repeat with the foot, to make a three-sided surround for the bed. The bed surround will now be reasonably stable, but it is advisable to position the long side against a wall. Paint the surround with pale grey emulsion.*

**two** *To stencil the bed linen, enlarge the templates on the next pages on to paper. Spray the backs lightly with spray adhesive and stick them on to sheets of stencil card. Cut out the stencils carefully, using a scalpel or craft knife on a cutting mat or sheet of thick card to protect your work surface. Peel off the paper patterns.*

**three** *Wash and iron the pillowcase to be stencilled. Place some paper inside the pillowcase. Position the first stencil, holding it in place with masking tape.*

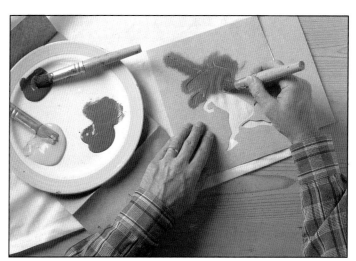

**four** *Spread each of the fabric paints on to the plate. Using a stencil brush, dab the first colour on to the pillowcase. Apply the paint sparingly as the colour is best when built up gradually.*

**five** *Position the next stencil, being very careful not to smudge the first one, and then stencil the second animal in another colour.*

**six** *Position a third stencil and apply the final colour. Continue alternating the stencils and colours to complete the pillowcase. Decorate the sheet or duvet cover in the same way.*

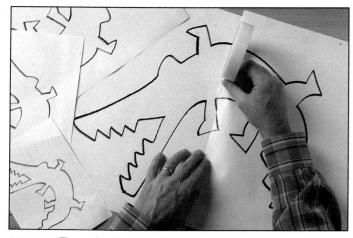

**seven** *To make the "window", enlarge the crocodile template in sections so that you end up with a good window-sized pattern. Then tape the different sections together. Rub the back of the pattern outline with a soft pencil.*

**eight** *Place the pattern face-up on the MDF and transfer by drawing over the outline with a hard pencil. Drill a hole at any point on the outline as the insertion point for the jigsaw blade.*

CONTINUED OVER ➤

**nine** *Use the jigsaw to cut out the crocodile shape. Work slowly and hold the blade vertically so that it cuts at its own speed without being pushed or dragged into the MDF. Rub down all the edges of the cut-out crocodile shape using fine-grade sandpaper.*

**ten** *Stencil a frieze of animals around the inside of the bed screen to co-ordinate with the bed linen. You can use the fabric paints for this, or matching stencil paints.*

# ROBOT CHAIR

A SIMPLE CHAIR MAY not suit a dramatic paint treatment, but you can add to basic chairs to create more height or add drama with a ladder-back effect. The easiest addition to use is already turned dowel, available from builders' merchants and DIY shops, which should be the thickness of your drill bit. If you are prepared for extra work in drilling out larger holes, all kinds of struts could be used, including twisted and carved pieces of the types used for shelving or balustrades. Decorating the chair with computer-age motifs in fluorescent paint adds further impact.

## YOU WILL NEED

ladder-back chair

pencil

drill, with wood drill bit

ruler or measuring tape

saw

wooden dowels

medium-grade sandpaper

hammer

royal blue emulsion paint

medium and fine paintbrushes

acrylic paint: white, fluorescent yellow, green and pink

permanent black marker

clear matt varnish

**one** *Mark the positions of the holes for the dowels. Drill all the holes. Keep the drill straight, or the dowel won't pass through both holes. Measure the back of the chair. Cut the dowels slightly longer than the chair back and sand the ends.*

**two** *Pass the dowel through one upright of the chair and line it up with the hole on the second upright.*

**three** *With a hammer, lightly tap the dowel through the second hole. Leave an equal amount of dowel showing on either side. Paint the whole chair with a blue base coat. Long, slow, even strokes will produce an even finish.*

**four** With a fine brush and white paint, sketch the outline for the "computer chip" design on the chair seat and on the wide struts of the back. The white provides a good base for the fluorescent paint. Again with a fine brush, paint on the design in yellow, green and pink fluorescent paints.

**five** Outline the design with the marker and add any further detail. Finally, to protect all the paintwork, coat the whole chair with clear varnish.

# SPACE BED

AT LAST, A TERRESTRIAL bed with all the glamour and sparkle of space travel. If the very thought of bedtime has the kids reaching for sci-fi videos, why not let them relax wrapped in their very own shimmering silver "space-blanket" beds? The shape of this headboard is reminiscent of a 1950s tail fin, but you can choose almost any bold shape that can be cut out of MDF with a jigsaw. You can buy "space blankets" from outdoor-supply shops.

## YOU WILL NEED

1 sheet MDF, width of the bed x height to bed base, plus approximately 1m (1yd)

pen

ruler

string

drawing pin

jigsaw

fine-grade sandpaper

polyester duvet

staple gun and staples

thin silver insulating material (the type used by athletes)

broad, woven adhesive tape

tape measure

thicker-textured silver insulating material (the type used under camping mattresses)

scissors

**one** *Draw a line across the width of the MDF about 40cm (16in) down from the top edge. Tie a 40cm (16in) length of string to a drawing pin and tie a pen to the other end. Push the pin into the line, just in from the left edge of the board. Pull the string taut and adjust its length to reach the top left-hand corner of the board. Using the string as the arm of a pair of compasses, draw a curve from the top of the board down to the horizontal line.*

**two** *Cut out the shape around the curve and along the line with a jigsaw. Sand down the edges.*

**three** *Fold the duvet around the MDF to give a smooth covering across the front. Fold the edges to the back.*

**four** *Staple the edges to the MDF, folding them under and tucking them in to get as even a finish as possible.*

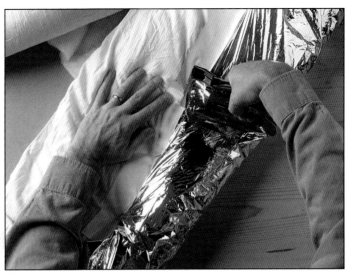

**five** *Lay the covered shape on to the thin silver insulating material. Fold the edges to the back and staple.*

**six** *Stick a strip of broad woven adhesive tape over the edges of the silver material to cover the staples and give a neat finish.*

**seven** *Turn the bedhead over and adjust any wrinkles in the "space blanket".*

**eight** *Mark points at intervals of 24cm (9½in) along a piece of string.*

**nine** *Use the piece of string to measure the positions of the quilting buttons on the covered headboard. Mark each point with a small square of woven tape.*

CONTINUED OVER ➤

**ten** *Cut strips of the thicker-textured insulating material into squares to use as "buttons" for the quilting.*

**eleven** *Staple a silver button on top of each tape square. Make sure that the silver covers up the tape. The tape strengthens the thin silver material and prevents the staples from tearing it.*

**twelve** *Push down hard with the staple gun, so that the staple penetrates right through to the MDF. Continue stapling the buttons in place until the whole headboard is quilted.*

# COMIC-STRIP CHAIR

THIS MONTAGE IDEA HAS bags of impact and could be adapted to many different themes. Here, we have chosen comic-strip characters to create a chair that would be welcome in the coolest teenager's bedroom. The seat cover could use any brightly coloured logo or graphic cut from fabric, or make use of a favourite image by taking a picture to a high street shop that transfers pictures on to T-shirts.

## YOU WILL NEED

wooden-framed chair

medium-grade sandpaper

scissors

paper motifs

wallpaper paste

paintbrushes

clear gloss varnish or
aerosol gloss varnish

blue stretchy fabric

staple gun

fabric logo (optional)

fabric adhesive (optional)

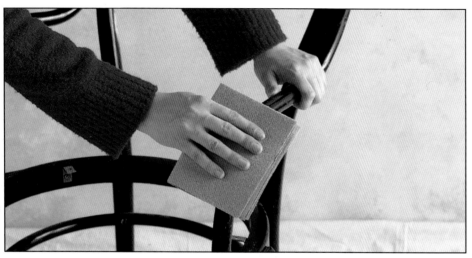

**one** *Remove the seat from the chair. Sand the chair lightly all over to provide a key for the paste. Cut out the motifs carefully with sharp-pointed scissors. Apply paste carefully all over the back of the motifs. Leave until tacky.*

**two** *Brush wallpaper paste over the chair frame, then apply the motifs to the chair, using a brush to prevent tearing them while they are wet. Repeat until you have covered the whole chair. Leave to dry.*

**three** *Apply a coat of varnish to protect the chair. For the seat cushion, stretch the fabric over the cushion and staple it in place. Pull the fabric taut as you work around the cushion. If you wish to decorate the seat further, find a logo or graphic to go in the centre. Apply fabric adhesive to the back and allow it to become tacky. Position and apply the logo to the seat cushion, pressing it down firmly until the glue has taken hold. Replace the cushion in the chair.*

# BOARD GAME CARPET

**ALONG WITH LINO TILES,** carpet tiles are real winners in the practicality stakes. Almost unbeatable in areas that need to be hardwearing and where children and their attendant wear and tear are concerned, carpet tiles have the single disadvantage that they never look like fitted carpet, no matter how well they are laid. Rather than fighting the fact that they come in non-fraying squares, make use of this very quality and create a fun floorscape, such as this giant board game. Carpet tiles are very forgiving, allowing for slight discrepancies in cutting and are very easy to replace if an area is damaged. A geometrical design is easiest; it is advisable to leave curves to the experts, but anything else, from a board game to the elegance of a painting by Mondrian, is accessible.

## YOU WILL NEED

metal tape measure

pencil

paper

carpet tiles

white crayon or white chinagraph pencil

metal ruler

rigid-bladed knife and plenty of spare blades

heavy duty, double-sided carpet tape

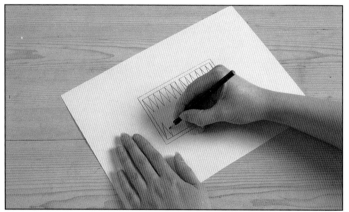

**one** *Measure your room and make sure that the floor is level and all protruding nails have been flattened. Any flat surface will accommodate the carpet tiles, whether it is marine-plywood, hardboard, floor boards or concrete. Plan your design on paper. Most rooms are not perfect rectangles so leave room for an area of plain tiles to edge the pattern.*

**two** *Measure the tiles, to determine the size of your pointed shapes and to work out how many tiles will be needed for your pattern. Consider the different weaves and nap of the carpet tiles, and make them work to enhance your chosen plan. Using a white crayon or chinagraph pencil, draw the pattern on the reverse of your tiles.*

◄

**three** *With a metal ruler and a rigid-bladed knife, score along the marked lines. Don't attempt to cut the tile through completely in one action. Starting at the top of the tile, cut down your scored lines. Do this on a solid surface and take extreme care while doing it.*

**four** *Lay down a line of carpet tape and remove the backing. Cut all the tiles for one complete run and fit these first, rather than laying little bits at a time.*

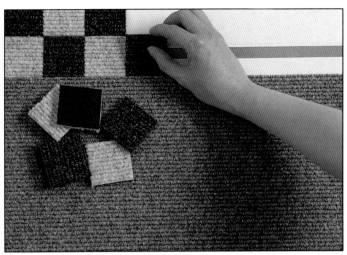

**five** *Stick your cut tiles in place, making sure not to pack them too tightly. Begin by making the whole of the checkered border. Then fill in, laying strips of carpet tape as you work. Tread the tiles down; uneven cuts will be unnoticeable.*

# MINIBUS TOYBOX

EVERY CHILD SHOULD BE ENCOURAGED to tidy away his or her toys at the end of the day. This eye-catching toybox might just do the trick! The pastel-coloured patches behind the bus stamps give the box a 1950s look. These are stencilled on to a light turquoise background. Stamp the buses on randomly so that some extend beyond the background shapes. Keep changing the angle of the stamp – the effect will be almost three-dimensional.

## YOU WILL NEED

hinged wooden box

emulsion paint: turquoise and three pastel colours

paintbrushes

stencil card and scalpel

4 plates

2 rollers

brown stamping ink and minibus stamp

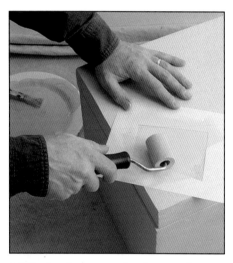

**one** *Apply two coats of turquoise emulsion paint to the box. Cut out the background shape stencil. It should be large enough for the whole stamp.*

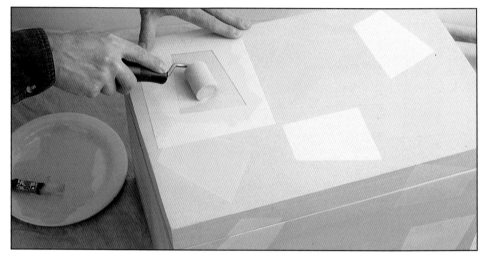

**two** *Spread the three pastel-coloured paints on plates. Roll the first colour through the stencil on to the box. You need a shape for each colour. Wash the roller and apply the two remaining colours, painting through the stencil as before. Balance the shapes with an equal amount of background colour. Leave to dry.*

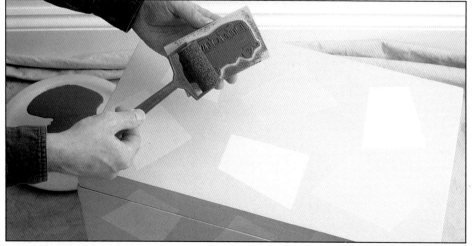

**three** *Pour some brown ink on to a plate. Coat the rubber stamp with the ink using a rubber roller. Stamp the bus motif on to the pastel background patches.*

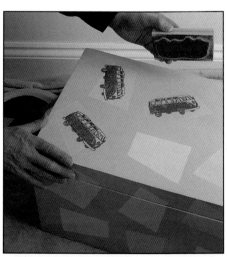

**four** *Allow the stamps to overlap the patches and vary the angle.*

# $\mathcal{B}$ATHROOMS

MOST PEOPLE'S IDEA OF an imaginatively-designed bathroom used to be stacking towels according to colour and arranging three empty perfume bottles on the windowsill. Not anymore. Bathrooms have come of decorating age, and deservedly so.

Bathrooms are a refuge from the cares of the world, where you can soak and pamper yourself with unashamed self-indulgence. But to get a bathroom that you actually want to spend quality time in, first you must pamper your surroundings.

Creams, white and washed-out pastels are always popular, and for good reason — they make small areas look larger. But there's no need to adhere blindly to white. What about, for example, a beach look?

Brightly-coloured metal beach buckets hung from a piece of driftwood should do the trick. You could cover a wall with plaster stars or create a mosaic splash-back of china. The view from the bath is looking better all the time!

What about views you don't want to see? Cover windows without losing light with fixed blinds made of translucently-coloured woven scrim, or strips of parched wood from a broken-up orange box — simple solutions that can be created in a matter of hours. And when night falls, turn off the cold overhead light and switch on the torch light.

*One idea to make your bathroom a bit unusual is to use bright buckets as containers. Buckets from the seaside will remind everyone of summer holidays!*

Three chrome torches fixed to a chrome rod to spotlight special items makes a spectacular effect.

Relegate the plastic laundry basket to the kids' room, and in its place put an antique-finished terracotta pot. To step over, rather than into, puddles of water on the floor, lay strips of raised wooden decking. It's easy and very practical.

The ideas in this chapter provide a bathroom in which you can wash, shower, bathe and unwind. Whether you go for the bright beach look, the classical Roman touch or the crisp, cool serenity of Japanese style, there will be just one problem — once inside, you'll never want to leave!

# BATHROOM BUCKETS

ADD AN ELEMENT OF seaside fun to your bathroom – as well as useful extra storage for all those odd-shaped items – by hanging up this row of bright buckets. This trio of enamel-painted buckets was bought from a toy shop, but you could take a trip to the seaside where you are bound to find a great selection of buckets in all shapes and sizes. While there, go for a stroll along the shore to find the ideal pieces of driftwood to fix to your wall.

## YOU WILL NEED

3 enamel-painted buckets
(or plastic seaside ones)
length of driftwood
(or an old plank)
pencil
drill, with wood and masonry bits
wire
pliers
wire cutters
masking tape
wall plugs and screws
screwdriver

**one** *Line the buckets up at equal distances along the wood. Make two marks, one at each end of the handle where it dips, for the three buckets. Using the wood bit, drill through the six marked positions to make holes through the wood.*

**two** *Wind wire round each handle end and poke it through the holes. Twist the two ends together at the back to secure. Trim the ends. Then drill a hole near each end of the wood.*

**three** *Hold the piece of wood in place and mark the positions for the fixings. Place a small piece of masking tape over the tile to prevent it from cracking, then drill the holes and fix the wood to the wall.*

# ꙄEA SHELL BOX

**BOXES DECORATED WITH** sea shells can be fairly awful, and unfortunately the worst ones have given this wonderfully relaxing pastime a bad name. But don't be put off – shells are naturally beautiful and there are endless ways of arranging them tastefully. This project combines the contemporary look of corrugated cardboard with a dynamic shell arrangement. For the finishing touch, the box is painted pure white matt.

## YOU WILL NEED

selection of sea shells

round corrugated cardboard box with lid

glue gun with all-purpose glue sticks (or all-purpose glue)

white acrylic paint (gesso primer is ultra white)

paintbrush

**one** *Lay out all the shells and sort them into different shapes and sizes. Arrange them on the lid to make the design. Remove the top layer of shells from the middle of the lid and begin sticking them on. Heat the glue gun and glue the outside shells first, gradually moving inwards.*

**two** *Work with the shell shapes, building up the middle section. The glue gun allows you to get an instant bond, so the shells will stick to the surface however you want them to.*

**three** *Paint the box and the lid white. If you are using acrylic gesso primer, two coats will give a good matt covering. If you are using ordinary acrylic or emulsion, the box will benefit from an extra coat of paint.*

# TERRACOTTA LAUNDRY POT

LAUNDRY IN A FLOWERPOT? It certainly sounds unusual, but this idea makes a refreshing change from the ubiquitous wicker basket in the bathroom. Terracotta pots are now available in a huge range of shapes and sizes and a visit to your local garden centre should provide you with just the right pot. To give a pristine pot an antique feel, follow these simple steps. This project would look good in a bathroom with a Mediterranean decor.

## YOU WILL NEED
large terracotta flowerpot
rag
shellac button polish
white emulsion paint
paintbrushes
scouring pad
sandpaper (optional)

**one** *Soak a rag in button polish and rub all over the surface of the pot with it. The polish will sink in very fast, leaving a yellow sheen.*

**two** *Mix white paint emulsion with an equal quantity of water. Stir it thoroughly and apply a coat to the pot. Allow the paint wash to dry.*

**three** *Rub the pot with the scouring pad to remove most of the white paint. The paint will cling to the crevices and along the mouldings to look like limescale. Either leave the pot like this or rub it back further with sandpaper to reveal the clay. When you are happy with the effect, apply a coat of button polish with a brush to seal the surface.*

# VICTORIAN STENCILLING

THIS IDEA ORIGINATED from the etched glass windows of the Victorian era. You can easily achieve the frosted, etched look on plain glass by using a stencil cut from stencil card and car enamel paint. The paint needs to be sprayed very lightly, so practise on some picture frame glass first to judge the effect. The stencil design is shown here, but you could easily design your own. Look at examples of lace panels to get some inspiration.

## YOU WILL NEED

tape measure

masking tape

tracing paper

stencil card

pencil

craft knife

brown paper

matt white car enamel spray

**one** *Measure the panes and mark the halfway points with masking tape. Photocopy and enlarge the stencil design and cut it from stencil card. Tape the main stencil pattern in position, then use brown paper to mask off the surrounding area, at least 50cm (20in) deep on all sides. (The spray spreads further than you think.)*

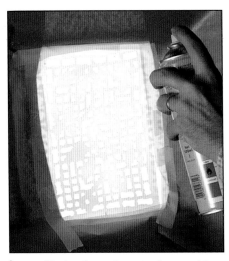

**two** *Shake the paint can thoroughly, as this affects the fineness of the spray. Spray from a distance of at least 30cm (12in), using short puffs of spray.*

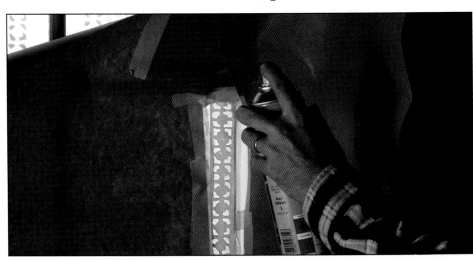

**three** *Depending on the dimensions of the window panes, there may be strips along the sides of the main panel that also need stencilling. This pattern has a border to fit around the edge – you may need to adapt it to fit your pane.*

# TORCH LIGHT

**A ROW OF ANGLED** chrome spotlights adds the designer touch to any shelf display, but wiring and fixing them can be a time-consuming and expensive undertaking, especially with the extra safety factors essential in a bathroom. Here is a way to obtain an even better effect without spending a lot of money or even plugging anything into the electrical circuit! All you need is three cheap chrome torches, a length of towel rail with sockets, a few fixtures and an hour to spare.

## YOU WILL NEED

3 small or medium chrome torches

3 small leather straps

pencil

hole punch

3 small jubilee clips

chrome shower rail with 2 sockets

screwdriver

drill, with masonry bit

wall plugs and screws

spirit level

**one** *Wrap a strap around a torch and mark the point where the buckle spike should enter. This will guarantee a good tight fit. Mark all the other straps in the same way.*

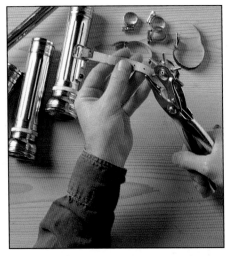

**two** *Punch a hole in each strap where marked.Slide the jubilee clips over the rail, loop a strap through each, then use a screwdriver to tighten the clips.*

**three** *Ensure that they are spaced evenly. Fit the rail into the sockets and fix these to the wall. Use a spirit level to ensure the rail is level before fixing. Buckle the torches to the rail.*

# ORANGE BOX BLIND

GREENGROCERS ARE ACCUSTOMED to supplying raw materials to their customers, but they might be a little surprised when you ask them for their wooden boxes rather than their fruit and vegetables! Get some orange boxes if you can, as the thin planks make ideal and original slats for blinds. These wooden blinds work best on a small, permanently obscurable window, such as in the bathroom. Although the blinds look Venetian, they don't actually pull up, but with a bit of perseverance you could probably make them do so. Here the wood was left natural, but it could be stained any colour.

## YOU WILL NEED

orange boxes

pliers

sharp knife

medium- and fine-grade
sandpaper

ruler

pencil

drill, and wood bit

string

scissors

2 cup hooks

**one** *Pull the orange boxes apart and select the most interesting parts from the longest sides. Remove any wire staples with pliers. Split some of the planks so that the slats are not all the same size. The final effect is more successful if the pieces are intentionally irregular.*

**two** *Shave off some of the wood to add character to the finished blind.*

**three** *Use medium-grade sandpaper first and then fine-grade sandpaper to smooth the wood and round off the edges.*

**four** *Place the slats side by side so that the edges line up. Mark a point 5cm (2in) from each end and 3cm (1¼in) from the bottom long edge. Although the slats are different widths, the holes should be drilled through points that line up on the front of the blind.*

**five** *Drill through the positions you have marked. The holes should be big enough to take the string through twice, but no bigger.*

**six** *Begin threading the string through the blind. Go through the blind from the back and pull a long length, about twice the drop of the window. It must be threaded all the way down the blind, to include all the looping around the slats.*

**seven** *Loop the string back over the slat and thread it through the hole a second time.*

◄

**eight** *Take the string up through the second slat. Continue as you did with the first, looping it around and through each slat twice, working all the way down the slats.*

CONTINUED OVER ➤

**nine** *When you get to the last slat, tie the string in a double knot and cut it off. Repeat this process on the other side. This is what the blind will look like from the "working side".*

**ten** *Turn the blind around as shown to hang it up so that you only see the string entering and leaving each slat. Screw two hooks up into the window frame and hang up the blind.*

# Mosaic Splashback

MOSAICS LOOK COMPLICATED and elaborate but are actually very simple to do; you just need time and patience to complete the job. Use up broken tiles or look for chipped junk-shop finds to make a unique splashback for behind a wash basin. You can have as simple or as complicated a colour scheme as you wish. You need a good selection of differently sized pieces. Break up the tiles, plates and so on by putting them between two pieces of cardboard and hammering them gently, but firmly. The cardboard will prevent tiny chips from flying around. Work on a piece of MDF so that you can sit down with the mosaic on a table, which is less back-breaking than applying the mosaic directly on to a wall.

## YOU WILL NEED

tape measure
MDF sheet
pencil
set square or ruler
jigsaw
drill, with wood and masonry bits
beading
mitre block and saw or mitre saw
wood glue
white emulsion paint
paintbrush
selection of broken tiles and ceramic fragments
glue gun and glue sticks
screws
grout
wall plugs
screwdriver

**one** *Measure the MDF to fit the width of your basin. Draw your chosen splashback shape on to the MDF using a pencil and a set square or ruler.*

**two** *Carefully cut out the shape using a jigsaw.*

**three** *Mark the position of the holes that will be used to attach the splashback to the wall. Drill the holes.*

**four** *Measure the beading that will frame the MDF. Mitre the beading using a mitre block or mitre saw.*

**five** *Glue the beading in place with wood glue, following the manufacturer's instructions.*

**six** *When the glue is dry, paint the whole splashback white. Leave to dry.*

**seven** *Arrange the ceramic pieces on the splashback. Experiment until you have created a pleasing pattern.*

**eight** *Glue the ceramic pieces in place using the glue gun.*

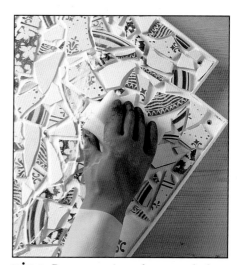

**nine** *Put screws into the screw holes, to prevent grout getting into the holes. Grout over the mosaic, being careful near any raised, pointed bits.*

CONTINUED OVER ➤

**ten** *Drill holes into the wall and insert the wall plugs. Then screw the splashback into position on to the wall.*

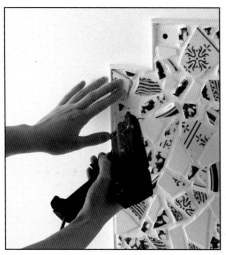

**eleven** *Glue on more ceramic pieces, to hide the screws.*

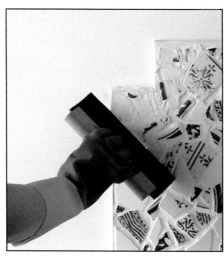

**twelve** *Re-grout over these pieces.*

# DECKING

**THE JAPANESE BATHHOUSE** is the inspiration for this floor treatment, preventing pools of water from turning your bathroom into a skating rink and, at the same time, imparting the serenity of a Zen garden. In this project the duckboards form a pontoon or walkway across the bathroom, but you could also use sections and cut them around the bathroom fittings. Ready-made decking is also available in strips or squares.

## YOU WILL NEED

tape measure

saw

quadrant beading

decking or duckboards

drill, with wood bit and pilot bit

soft cloth

paintbrush

wood stain

wood screws

**one** *Make sure you have a clean, level floor: cork tiles, wood and lino are all suitable. The existing floor will show through, so if you want to change the colour, do so now! Measure and cut the two lengths of beading to the same length as the runners on the decking or duckboards. Drill holes through these new runners. Stain the two new long runners to the same colour as the decking or duckboards.*

**two** *Measure the distance between the runners on the decking or duckboard.*

**three** *Space the new runners at a distance that will allow the decking or duckboard runners to slide between them, holding the board steady but allowing it to be lifted up for cleaning. Screw in place by drilling through the subfloor, using the correct type of bit for the type of floor you have. Slide the boards into place.*

# PATCHWORK EFFECT TILES

**BATHROOMS AND SHOWER ROOMS** are often thought of simply as basic utility rooms because they tend to get heavily splashed and also, with today's busy lifestyle, most people spend little time there. Consequently, their floorings are frequently correspondingly spartan. However, the wide range of ceramic tiles now available enables you to achieve stunning good looks without sacrificing practicality. Here we opted for stylish blue tiles in the same colour range, accented by deep indigo.

## YOU WILL NEED
pencil

ruler

tile adhesive (waterproof for bathrooms; flexible if on a suspended floor)

ceramic tiles

notched spreader

tile spacers

straight edge (optional)

squeegee

grout

damp sponge

lint-free dry cloth

dowel scrap

**one** *Draw a grid on the floor for the tiles. Using the spreader, spread some adhesive on an area of the floor small enough to be reached easily. Start laying the tiles. As you do so, use spacers to ensure that the gaps between them are even. Use a straight edge to check that all the tiles are horizontal and level. When all the tiles have been laid, use a squeegee to spread grout over them and fill all the join lines – this is for both appearance and waterproofing.*

**two** *Wipe off the surplus grout with a damp sponge before it dries.*

**three** *Buff with a dry cloth when the grout has hardened, then smooth the grout with the scrap piece of dowel.*

# WOVEN BLIND

THIS COLOURED MESH RIBBON is one of the new natural materials now available. It is stiff enough to hold its shape and be folded into sharp creases to make a blind. Use this treatment for a window that must be be obscured from prying eyes while still allowing maximum light to penetrate the room – a bathroom, shower room or toilet. To make the most of their interesting texture and soft colours, the ribbons have been interwoven.

## YOU WILL NEED

strips of woven mesh ribbon
in 3 colours, 6cm (2½in)
wide

scissors

tape measure

2 broom handles

staple gun

bradawl

2 plumbers' pipe fittings

screwdriver

**one** *Cut lengths of woven mesh ribbon to the length of the drop, plus 20cm (8in). Wrap a 10cm (4in) length around a broom handle and secure it with a staple gun. Leaving 3cm (1¼in) gaps between each ribbon, continue fixing the ribbons along the broom handle with the staple gun. Finish with 9cm (3½in) of bare wood at the end. Repeat this process to fix the ends of the strips to the second broom handle.*

**two** *Cut the remaining two colours into strips to fit the width of the blind, plus a 3cm (1¼in) allowance each side. Weave these through the first ribbons.*

**three** *At each side, turn the seam over and crease it with your thumbnail, then staple the two ribbons together. Use a bradawl to make two small holes on either side of the underside of the top recess, then screw in the plumbers' fittings. Put the broom handle in position, then screw the front section of the fittings into position.*

# Hand-Printed "Tiles"

These imitation tiles are, in fact, hand-printed on to the wall using a home-made foam stamp. This is a quicker and less expensive alternative to ceramic tiles, and there are endless colour combinations. If you opt for tones of one colour, it is inexpensive because you can buy one pot of paint and lighten it with white to achieve different tones. Making a sponge stamp to apply the colour is a quick and foolproof way of getting squares of colour on to the wall. If you start with a white wall, the lines left between the fake tiles will look like the grouting between real tiles.

### YOU WILL NEED
ruler
pencil
scrap paper
high-density foam
glue
craft knife
self-healing cutting mat
emulsion paint in 2 colours, plus white
paintbrushes
scissors
straight edge
spirit level
old plates
small roller
small brush
clear varnish
varnish brush

**one** *Decide on the size of the tiles. Draw your design for the stamp on paper. Glue it to the foam and cut out unwanted areas. Angle the cut outwards slightly from top to bottom. Make a stamp for each colour. For this design you need six stamps.*

**two** *Use smaller pieces of foam to make a handle on the back of each stamp.*

**three** *Choose your colours – aquatic greens and blues work particularly well in bathrooms. Here, a scheme of six tones, made from two basic colours, was used. One-third of each colour was mixed together to make a third colour, and then these three colours were halved again and lightened with white.*

**four** *Decide on the repeat pattern; small-scale paper squares, painted in the different colours and/or tones, will help you plan the design.*

**five** *Mark horizontal guidelines on the wall with faint pencil lines, using a straight edge and a spirit level.*

**six** *Mark vertical guidelines in the same way.*

**seven** *Put some paint on to a plate and run the roller through it until it is evenly coated, then roll the paint on to the first stamp.*

CONTINUED OVER ➤

**eight** *Stamp the "tile" pattern on to the wall, pressing down firmly with your fingers. Go right around the "grout" area and touch up any stray smudges with white paint and a small brush. Make sure that no pencil guidelines are visible.*

**nine** *When dry, apply two coats of varnish to protect the surface and give it a wipeable finish.*

# PLASTER STARS

PLASTER HAS A POWDERY quality and a pure white colour, which make it an especially interesting wall embellishment. Equally, of course, it can be painted in any colour of your choice. Most decorative plaster firms have lots of simple shapes – both modern and traditional – to choose from and will make a mould of virtually anything you like, so the possible variations of this effect are endless. This idea works well as a border above a skirting board or around a door, as well as in a defined area, such as behind a wash basin, as shown here.

## YOU WILL NEED
plaster stars
scissors
masking tape
PVA glue or clear varnish
paintbrush
wall adhesive
wood offcut

**one** *Decide on the design and spacing of the stars (or the fancy plaster motifs of your choice) by making photocopies of them, cutting them out and using small pieces of masking tape to attach them to the wall. Try out a number of versions until you are happy with the final effect.*

**two** *Seal the stars with clear varnish or PVA glue mixed with water.*

**three** *When the stars are dry, use wall adhesive to attach them to the walls. Use a wood offcut as a spacer for positioning the stars on the wall.*

# GREEK KEY BATHROOM

This bathroom looks far too smart to have been decorated by an amateur. The border design is a classic Greek key interspaced with a bold square and across. The black and gold look stunning on a pure white tiled wall. Every bathroom has different features, so use the border to make the most of the best ones, while drawing attention away from the duller areas. If you want a co-ordinated scheme, you could print a border on a set of towels, using fabric inks.

## YOU WILL NEED

tracing paper

pencil

spray adhesive

high-density foam, such as upholstery foam

scalpel

acrylic enamel paint: black and gold

2 plates

wooden baton 2-3cm/³⁄4-1¹⁄4in wide, depending on the bathroom

masking tape

**one** *Trace and transfer the pattern shapes from the template. Lightly spray the shapes with adhesive and place them on the foam. To cut out the shapes, cut the outline first, then undercut and remove any excess, leaving the pattern shape standing proud of the foam.*

**two** *Apply an even coating of black paint on to a plate. Place the baton up next to the door frame to keep the border an even distance from it. Make a test print on scrap paper, then begin by stamping one black outline square in the bottom corner, at dado-rail height. Print a key shape above it, being careful not to smudge the adjoining edge of the previous print.*

**three** *Continue alternating the stamps around the door. Mark the base line at the dado-rail height with masking tape and alternate the designs along this line.*

**four** *Place a coating of gold paint on to a plate and dip the cross shape into it. Make a test print on scrap paper, then print the shape in the square frames.*

*Maths montage page 76*

*Country-style shelf page 94*

5

5 ²

3  +

M ) = 8

*Escher-style wall page 78*

*Sprigged calico curtains page 54*

*Director's chair page 36*

*Flag stencils page 194*

*Trompe-l'oeil linoleum page 112*

*Vermeer-style marble page 114*

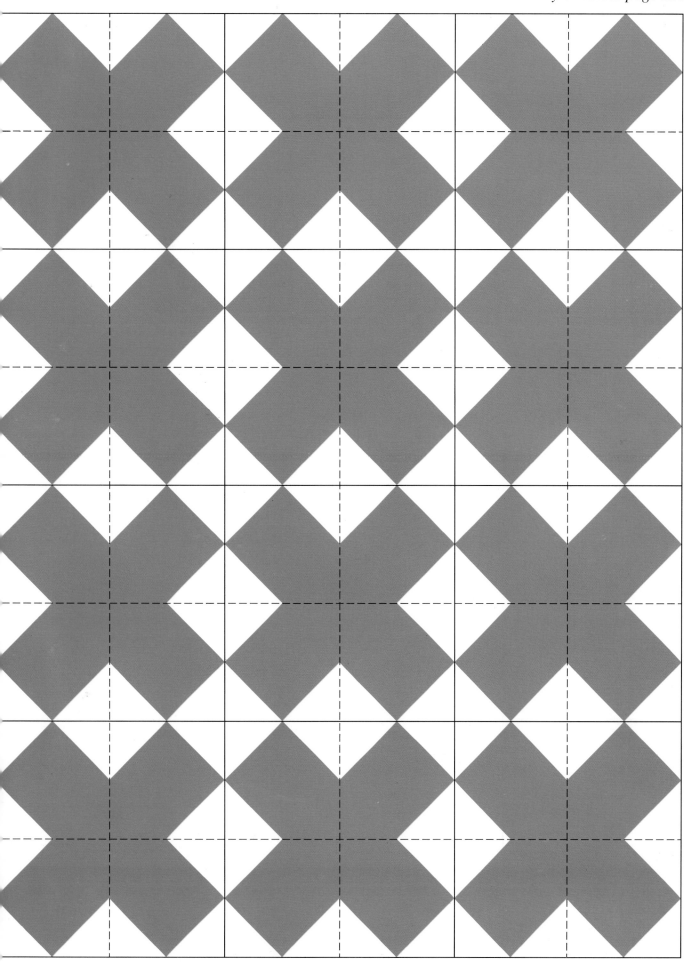

# INDEX

American dream, 168-9

antique map, 74-5

armchairs:
  jewel-bright armchair, 48-9
  Wild West chair, 62-3

basket, beaded laundry, 198-9

bathroom buckets, 218-19

bathrooms, 216-49

battens, coloured wooden, 24-5

beaded laundry basket, 198-9

bed covers, sheer magic, 172-3

bedheads:
  corrugated headboard, 184-5
  Indian temple bedhead, 158-9
  space bed, 206-9

bedrooms, 134-89

beds:
  four-poster sari, 160-1
  half-tester, 146-9

billowing muslin, 182-3

blackboard, wall, 192-3

blinds:
  hessian and scrim blinds,
    128-31

  orange box blind, 228-31
  woven blind, 240-1

board game carpet, 212-13

bold blocks of colour, 50-1

borders:
  Greek key bathroom, 248-9
  pistachio-shell border, 162-3
  plaster stars, 246-7

boxes:

cutlery box, 110-11
  seashell box, 220-1
  toy box, 214-15
  window box shelf, 98-9

brick "tiles", painted, 126-7

buckets:
  bathroom buckets, 218-19
  toy box, 214-15

builders' scrim, textured gold
floor, 166-7

butterfly montage, 180-1

calico:
  calico tent, 174-7
  sprigged curtains, 54-5

calligraphy:
  copycats, 154-5
  stamps and dry brush, 142-3

candle-wrappers, the new wave,
  186-7

candleholders, shell, 178-9

cardboard see corrugated card
  board

carpet tiles, board game carpet,
  212-13

ceramic pieces, mosaic splash
  back, 232-5

chairs:
  colourful kitchen chair, 106-7
  comic-strip chair, 210-11
  dining chair, 42-3
  draped director's chair, 36-7
  Eastern promise, 68-9
  Escher's deckchair, 80-1
  gilded chair, 150-1
  Gustavian chair, 152-3
  jewel-bright armchair, 48-9
  laced dining chair, 38-41
  minimalist chair, 72-3
  pull-down stool, 86-9
  robot chair, 204-5
  Wild West chair, 62-3

child's bedroom nook, 200-3

Chinese lantern, 144-5

circles, decorative, 84-5

colour-washed parquet, 26-7

coloured wooden battens, 24-5

comic-strip chair, 210-11

contemporary shelf, 58-9

copper tube:
  calico tent, 174-7
  standard paint cans, 70-1

copycats, 154-5

corrugated cardboard and paper:
  Chinese lantern, 144-5
  corrugated headboard, 184-5
  corrugated lampbase, 188-9
  the new wave, 186-7

country-style shelf, 94-5

crates, Mediterranean, 96-7

cream topping, 12-13

curtains:
  billowing muslin, 182-3
  drawing-room secrets, 30-1
  half-tester, 146-9
  no-frills navy, 32-3
  purple playroom, 196-7
  shell shocked, 170-1
  sprigged curtains, 54-5

curving rope design, 18-19

cushions, life's little luxuries,
  20-1

cut-above tiles, 108-9

cutlery box, 110-11

deckchair, Escher's, 80-1

decking, 236-7

decorative circles, 84-5

dining chair, 42-3
  laced dining chair, 38-41

dining rooms, 8-59

director's chairs:
  draped director's chair, 36-7
  Eastern promise, 68-9

distressed floorboards, 56-7

doorway, Tuscan, 122-5

draped director's chair, 36-7

drawing-room secrets, 30-1

driftwood:
  bathroom buckets, 218-19
  driftwood and pebble frames,
    178-9

dry brush technique, 142-3

dustpan tidy, 66-7

dustsheets, Japanese futon,
  140-1

Eastern promise, 68-9

Escher-style wall, 78-9

Escher's deckchair, 80-1

filigree wooden panel, 164-5

flags:
  American dream, 168-9
  flag stencils, 194-5

floating floor, 52-3

floors:
  butterfly montage, 180-1
  colour-washed parquet, 26-7
  decking, 236-7
  distressed floorboards, 56-7
  groovy floor, 46-7
  parquet, 44-5
  patchwork effect tiles, 238-9
  pistachio-shell border, 162-3
  sheet-metal tread mats, 132-3
  stamps and dry brush, 142-3
  textured gold floor, 166-7
  trompe l'oeil linoleum, 112-13
  Vermeer-style marble, 114-17

flowerpots, terracotta laundry
  pot, 222-3

four-poster sari, 160-1

frames:
  driftwood and pebble frames,
    178-9
  the new wave, 186-7

futon, Japanese, 140-1

geometric wall-board, 28-9
gilded chair, 150-1
gold floor, textured, 166-7
Greek key bathroom, 248-9
groovy floor, 46-7
Gustavian chair, 152-3

half-tester, 146-9
hallways, 60-91
hand-printed "tiles", 242-5
hanging jam jars, 100-1
hanging rack, trellis, 82-3
headboards:
  corrugated headboard, 184-5
  Indian temple bedhead, 158-9
  space bed, 206-9
hessian and scrim blinds, 128-31

Indian summer, 156-7
Indian temple bedhead, 158-9

jam jars, hanging, 100-1
Japanese futon, 140-1
Japanese screen, 138-9
jewel-bright armchair, 48-9

kelims, Eastern promise, 68-9
kitchens, 92-133

laced dining chair, 38-41
lamps:
  Chinese lantern, 144-5
  corrugated lampbase, 188-9
  lime-washed lamp base, 22-3
  mutton cloth shade, 16-17
  primary plastic, 34-5
  skewbald shade, 64-5
  standard paint cans, 70-1
  string-bound lamp base, 14-15
  torch light, 226-7
  tripod light, 136-7
laundry:
  beaded laundry basket, 198-9
  terracotta laundry pot, 222-3
life's little luxuries, 20-1
lights see lamps
lime-washed lamp base, 22-3
linocut stamps, sprigged
  curtains, 54-5
linoleum, trompe l'oeil, 112-13
living rooms, 8-59

map, antique, 74-5
marble, Vermeer-style, 114-17
maths montage, 76-7
Mediterranean crates, 96-7
metal:
  sheet-metal tread mats, 132-3
  toy box, 214-15
minimalist chair, 72-3
mirror, driftwood and pebble
  frame, 178-9
montages:
  butterfly montage, 180-1
  maths montage, 76-7
mosaic splashback, 232-5
muslin, billowing, 182-3
mutton cloth shade, 16-17

necklace, pebble and stone,
  178-9
the new wave, 186-7
newspapers, on the shelf,
  120-1
no-frills navy, 32-3
noticeboard, wooden, 118-19
novelty rooms, 190-215

on the shelf, 120-1
orange box blind, 228-31

paint cans, standard lamp, 70-1
painted brick "tiles", 126-7
pallets, Japanese futon, 140-1
parquet, 44-5
  colour-washed parquet, 26-7
patchwork effect tiles, 238-9
pebble and stone necklace,
  178-9
pelmets:
  cream topping, 12-13
  drawing-room secrets, 30-1

photocopies:
  copycats, 154-5
  cut-above tiles, 108-9
  flag stencils, 194-5
  maths montage, 76-7
picture frames:
  driftwood and pebble, 178-9
  the new wave, 186-7
pillows:
  American dream, 168-9
  sheer magic, 172-3
pistachio-shell border, 162-3
plaster stars, 246-7
plastic, primary, 34-5
playroom, purple, 196-7
potato stamps, contemporary
  shelf, 58-9
pretty kitchen chair, 106-7
primary plastic, 34-5
pull-down stool, 86-9
punched tin, toy box, 214-15
purple playroom, 196-7

quilts, American dream, 168-9

racks:
  trellis hanging rack, 82-3
  vegetable rack, 102-5

radiator panelling, filigree
  wooden panel, 164-5
raffia, on the shelf, 120-1
robot chair, 204-5
Roman blind, hessian and scrim,
  128-31
rope:
  cream topping, 12-13
  curving rope design, 18-19
  rope-trimmed cushion cover,
  20

super sofa, 10-11

sari lengths:
  four-poster sari, 160-1
  Indian summer, 156-7
screens:
  child's bedroom nook, 200-3
  Japanese screen, 138-9
scrim:
  hessian and scrim blinds,
  128-31
  textured gold floor, 166-7
seashell box, 220-1
seaside setting, 178-9

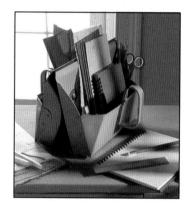

sheer magic, 172-3
sheet-metal tread mats, 132-3
shells:
  seashell box, 220-1
  shell candleholders, 178-9
  shell shocked, 170-1
shelves:
  contemporary shelf, 58-9
  country-style shelf, 94-5
  hanging jam jars, 100-1
  on the shelf, 120-1
  window box shelf, 98-9
skewbald shade, 64-5
slip covers:
  draped director's chair, 36-7
  laced dining chair, 38-41
sofa, super, 10-11
space bed, 206-9
splashback, mosaic, 232-5
spotlights, torch light, 226-7
sprigged curtains, 54-5
stamps:
  billowing muslin, 182-3
  contemporary shelf, 58-9
  country-style shelf, 94-5

Escher's deckchair, 80-1
hand-printed "tiles", 242-5
sprigged curtains, 54-5
stamps and dry brush, 142-3
standard paint cans, 70-1
stars, plaster, 246-7
stationery, dustpan tidy, 66-7
stencils:
child's bedroom nook, 200-3
flag stencils, 194-5
geometric wall-board, 28-9
skewbald shade, 64-5
Victorian stencilling, 224-5
stool, pull-down, 86-9
string:
on the shelf, 120-1
string-bound lamp base, 14-15
studies, 60-91
sun-lounger, 90-1
super sofa, 10-11

tent, calico, 174-7
terracotta laundry pot, 222-3
textured gold floor, 166-7
tiles:
cut-above tiles, 108-9
hand-printed "tiles", 242-5
mosaic splashback, 232-5
painted brick "tiles", 126-7

patchwork effect tiles, 238-9
tin punching, toy box, 214-15
tongue-and-groove boards,
groovy floor, 46-7
torch light, 226-7
towels, copycats, 155
toy box, 214-15
trellis:
Japanese screen, 138-9
trellis hanging rack, 82-3
trimmings, on the shelf, 120-1
tripod light, 136-7
trompe l'oeil linoleum, 112-13
Tuscan doorway, 122-5
typist's chair, minimalist chair,
72-3
vegetable rack, 102-5
Vermeer-style marble, 114-17

Victorian stencilling, 224-5
voile, sheer magic, 172-3

walls:
antique map, 74-5
bold blocks of colour, 50-1
coloured wooden battens,
24-5
curving rope design, 18-19
decorative circles, 84-5
Escher-style wall, 78-9
filigree wooden panel, 164-5
geometric wall-board, 28-9
Greek key bathroom, 248-9
maths montage, 76-7
painted brick "tiles", 126-7
plaster stars, 246-7
shell shocked, 170-1

wall blackboard, 192-3
webbing, sun-lounger, 90-1
Wild West chair, 62-3
window box shelf, 98-9
windows:
billowing muslin, 182-3
cream topping, 12-13
drawing-room secrets, 30-1
Indian summer, 156-7
no-frills navy, 32-3
purple playroom, 196-7
Victorian stencilling, 224-5
wood:
colour-washed parquet, 26-7
coloured wooden battens,
24-5
decking, 236-7
distressed floorboards, 56-7
filigree wooden panel, 164-5
floating floor, 52-3
groovy floor, 46-7
Mediterranean crates, 96-7
orange box blind, 228-31
parquet, 44-5
window box shelf, 98-9
wooden noticeboard, 118-19
woven blind, 240-1
wrapping paper, copycats,
154